An Inquiry into
the Nature and Causes of

THE WEALTH
OF PEOPLE

An Inquiry into
the Nature and Causes of

THE WEALTH
OF PEOPLE

Martin Gerhard Giesbrecht

William Kaufmann, Inc.
One First Street
Los Altos, California

Library of Congress Cataloging in Publication Data

Giesbrecht, Martin Gerhard, 1933-
    An Inquiry into the Nature and Causes of the Wealth of People

    1. Economics. I. Title.
HB171.5.G453   330   73-19520
ISBN 0-913232-11-4

Table of Contents

Preface

Times change. Sometimes they change with much celebration or with the loud bang of a "future shock". But mostly they seem to change stealthily, quickly and quietly, and we suddenly find ourselves in a new world without even having noticed when the old one disappeared. Either way, with or without noisy announcement, we often find ourselves facing today's brand new problems armed only with yesterday's outdated wisdom and obsolete tools.

Science—including economic science—suffers from this malady too. Of course, as long as the scientific process is rational and deductive, our scientific tools must always be forged out of past, not future, experiences. But beyond this, conventional economic wisdoms seem to have a way of hanging on. Too often modern economics seems reduced to fighting the battles of past wars, or, in less historic terms, to chasing parked cars.

One response to this obsolescence—the response incorporated in most of today's introductory economics textbooks—is to counsel patience, to point out that new ideas are being developed on the frontiers of the science and that these will trickle down to everybody else in due time. The trouble with this, obviously, is that most of us are not patient. Furthermore, to learn an obsolete science is also to reinforce and perpetuate it, since we tend to teach what we have learned.

Another response to obsolescence is to advocate a radical break with convention. The appeal of such a drastic measure grows as the frustration with the old convention mounts, and revolutions in science and in economics do happen. But the trouble with revolutions is that they are blunt instruments that often destroy more than necessary. Even worse, they usually establish a new convention that seems as happy to descend into comfortable obsolescence as the old.

The purpose of this book is to make a new departure from all this. It is neither a revolutionary tract nor a recitation of obsolete orthodoxy. Rather, I like to think of it as a look at today's economic processes with new perceptions. Much of what we see, of course, has been seen before and is familiar stuff to conventional economics. But much that we see is quite new. Most importantly, be they familiar or new, when seen with fresh eyes the economic processes themselves reveal the new visions and new analyses we are seeking for our times.

For one thing, we see that economic processes are not mechanical, but are organic and evolutionary. As part of life itself, they flow along time's arrow towards entropy. For another, while the determining forces and boundaries of economic processes may be interpreted differently by different ideologies, we see that ideology does not establish these forces and boundaries definitively. Instead, we see that a kind of physical "realeconomics" works beneath the obscuring dichotomy of "capitalism vs. communism", allowing us to understand both "isms" better with one mind and one analytical perspective. Furthermore, we see that economic processes contain much more than the commercial production, market, and monetary matters dealt with almost exclusively by conventional economics. Especially the intrafamilial, social, environmental and population concerns that economic orthodoxy has labeled "externalities", or has consigned to noneconomic status, seem very much to be "centralities" in the real economic concerns of today. And even inflation, unemployment, the concentration of economic power, economic development, and many other conventional economic issues seem to take on more recognizably realistic shapes when seen in this new light.

So is this new departure a framework for the basic understanding of economics in all future times and places? As tempted as I might be to dare to hope so, I am sure it must, sooner or later, share the fate of all other paradigms before it. But in the meantime, I permit myself the hope that it is a superior way to make an introductory inquiry into the nature and causes of the wealth of people today—and for part of tomorrow too.

Acknowledgments

Certainly most of the analyses and ideas in this book are derived from others. My teachers, especially Monroe Berkowitz, Leopold Kohr, and Broadus Mitchell of Rutgers University, Edward Chamberlin of Harvard University, and Alfred von Martin at the University of Munich; my friends and colleagues, especially the august members of the Social Science Forum at Wilmington College; the many writers whose works have influenced me strongly, including especially Kenneth Boulding of the University of Colorado, Edgar S. Dunn, Jr. of Resources for the Future, Inc., Nicholas Georgescu-Roegen of Vanderbilt University, and the recently deceased Jacques Monod of the Pasteur Institute, among my contemporaries; and my students, whose hunger for a relevant economics spurred me on to this effort; all have had a hand in it. Most of them were quite unaware of their participation, of course, and they may hardly recognize their good ideas in these altered forms and contexts. I am particularly grateful for the help on the manuscript received from Kenneth Boulding, Herman E. Daly of Louisiana State University, Sidney Wertimer, Jr. of Hamilton College, Lawrence E. Leamer of the State University of New York at Binghamton, and Carol Berge, Estelle Jelinek, J. M. B. Edwards, and Sarah Rush, all of the San Francisco area. Most particularly I am grateful to Bill Kaufmann the publisher, a gracious man, whose personal commitment to his books is both a joy and an example to their authors.

To Lisa,
  Marty, and
  Ted

CHAPTER 1

The Human Economic System

Once Over the Economy Lightly.

Let us begin by celebrating something pleasant on which we can all agree. Let us toast to ourselves, that we are alive and thinking and dreaming. Let us simply cheer the fact that we are here.

Our presence is, after all, a most unusual state of affairs in the universe. Not only does human life seem to be unique to our small planet, but we are beginning to find that life itself seems to be a rare occurence on any planet, perhaps even in any galaxy. Indeed, the existence of *anything* in the vastness of infinite space and time is a fleeting occurence, since all things, all masses, and all energies tend to disperse. to spend themselves, and eventually to scatter through all the dimensions of the universe. In time, rocks will be ground to sand, mountains will fill in the seas, the seas will evaporate, and the sun will dim out and die. This inescapable future makes it all the more marvelous, then, that our beautiful universe of matter and energy, of stars, planets, and the gorgeous earth *does* exist now and that we exist now too, so that we can perceive at least some of these glories.

I assume that the vast majority of the objects in the universe today are unaware of their own good fortune in this matter. Apparently rocks, mountains, and seas have no consciousness. Only a very few of all the things in our world clearly participate actively in their own existence. They seem to be purposely striving to use the materials and energies in their environment to survive and to sustain themselves. We distinguish these from all the rest by calling them "alive", and we honor the distinction by making this striving, as it applies to ourselves, the ultimate focus of much of our personal attention and much of our cultural wisdom. This focus is called economics.

Of course,there is more to human life than economics, than survival and sustenance. Love, power, status, sex—our poets and philosophers can supply us with a more complete list—play varied but essential roles in our lives. But we will find that the economic process is almost always inextricably intertwined with all of these. For example, wealth, which we usually think of as an object of rather economic concern, is an important instrument for achieving those very aforementioned noneconomic ends: love, power, status, and sex. To quote an observant friend, "Romance without finance is a nuisance!" Human motives are typically complex; therefore the activities and processes that serve these motives are not easily isolated from one another. And we can be sure that economics will almost always be involved, because confirming life—a good life, we hope, perhaps even an exuberant one—is what economics is all about.

Our economic lives cannot be carried out in a vacuum. Like all living things, we need an environment sufficiently beneficent to supply and resupply us with fresh matter and energy. These resources are in the form of anything and everything that we find useful and available. Specifically included are all categories of natural resources: minerals and fuels found in the ground, forests, land, bodies of water, climate, air space, solar and gravitational energies, whatever we find in outer space, and so on. Also included are all the living earthly flora and fauna, the trees, grasses, fish, insects, birds, and animals. And emphatically included are we ourselves. Our society, our culture, and even our bodies and minds are the most important resources in our environment. Quite literally, anything of which we can avail ourselves—

whether it is tangible or intangible, naturally occurring or artificially created—is a resource for the supply and resupply of our economic process.

Like all processes, the economic process is entropic. By this is meant that life contributes to the wearing out of energies and materials. For example, such natural concentrations as coal, petroleum, iron ore, alluvial soils, and fresh river water, as well as our own mental and physical substance, are not yet dissipated or exhausted when they are first drawn into the economic process. As we use them, however, we tend to use them up, to pollute them, and to wear them out. We *increase* their entropy. The most useful parts of our environment, then, are still in a state of *low* entropy. Low entropy indicates high potential. The entropic economic process consumes that potential and, in doing so, increases entropy.

Sometimes economic activity aims intentionally to alter the environment, so that future economic activity will be more effective and efficient. This beneficial alteration of the environment is achieved by various kinds of accumulation. For example, "accumulating" industrial tools and equipment, or accumulating technical knowledge and other skill are all means of enhancing the efficiency of our future economic activity. It even makes sense to speak of "accumulating" a healthy and energetic population—us—for this purpose.

The measure of success of the economic process is the same measure used in all aspects of life; call it "satisfaction", for the lack of a better word. It may be the grim satisfaction of simple survival, or it may be the delight of increasing our health, wealth, comfort, and life span. It may be the satisfaction of achieving a high level of material consumption, or it may be the satisfaction of doing well in comparison to others. Personal feelings of security, identity, achievement, or adventure may be a major part of it, as may be communal or nationalist goals, such as economic development and power. Whatever form it takes and as elusive and immeasurable as it may be, satisfaction remains the best perceptible common denominator of economic success, at least, for our purposes in this book.

Just like the well-known chicken-and-egg sequence, the economic process has no beginning and no end. It is ongoing, from day to day and generation to generation, and feedbacks and sequential chains of events abound. For example, we have just seen that satisfaction is the goal of the economic process. Yet, in order to carry on the activities of the economic process—production, consumption, ownership, and exchange—an expenditure of human energy is required. This energy must be derived from the pool of human strength and well-being that is itself a major source of satisfaction for us, with the result that the sum total of our satisfaction is depleted by the very process that created it in the first place. So, it seems that we work to eat, but we also have to eat to work. And notice that the two are very strongly linked: the one *requires* the other. And thus, the economic process continues. Pessimists might decry the futility of it all; optimists will recognize herein the joyous fulfillment of life itself.

So far, then, our economic process may be portrayed as follows:

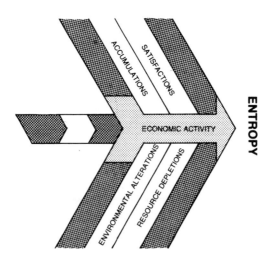

Figure A: The Economic Process Through Time

This picture shows us that our striving to live and to live well leads to satisfactions and the accumulation of productivity enhancing wealth, in the course of time. Our environment is also altered, resources are depleted, and the entropy of the whole system is increased.

Notice that no mention is made yet of goods and services, no mention of taxes or unemployment, not even any mention of MONEY! And the whole system is not circular. It does not come back on itself to go around once again. It just proceeds through time like Omar Khayyam's "moving finger," which, "having writ, Moves on:".

Pictures and diagrams of the economic process should be considered like snapshots in a family photo album. Each one shows us a different scene. No single one can tell the whole story in all its details. But taken together in the album, the pictures can portray rather accurately what the family really was like. In the course of this book, I will show nine more pictures of various aspects of the economy, in various poses, and from various perspectives. The next snapshot is taken from closer-up and shows greater detail.

Economic Transformations.

What do we do when we are engaged in economic activity? We *transform* things. This is the most all-inclusive and general statement we can make about it. For instance, we transform things from raw materials into finished products, from finished products into consumer satisfactions, and from consumer satisfactions into energy for more economic activity again. The process is depicted in some detail in Figure B.

In a loose way, this diagram represents the outline of the remainder of this book, because we can come to understand economics by understanding each of the transformations. However, in order not to lose sight of the whole, it might be a good idea to describe each of the transformations and suggest how they fit together now.

The first one, the PROPRIETARY TRANSFORMATION, is a change in ownership only and does not constitute any real change of physical substance. Its arrow is drawn with

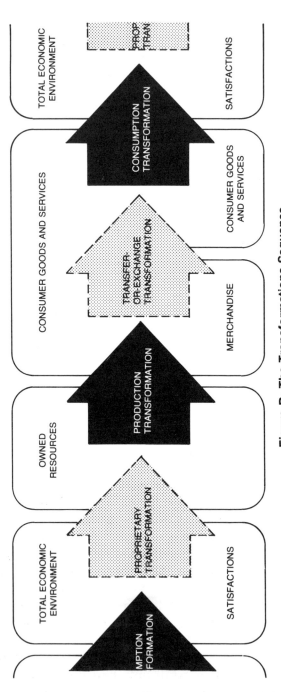

Figure B: The Transformations Sequence

broken lines to indicate this. The proprietary transformation simply signals that a part of the environment has been claimed by an individual or group of individuals as a resource for economic purposes.

The second one, the PRODUCTION TRANSFORMA-TION, carries the raw economic resource all the way through to the finished product. This includes a great many steps and changes that are not detailed by the figure above. For example, if we consider a brand-new automobile sitting in the dealer's show room, the production transformation would have to include digging iron ore out of the ground, drilling and pumping for oil to be made into fuels, plastics, and textiles; processing steel; stamping, forging, and machining parts; running an assembly line; using technology, managerial efforts, and accumulations of machinery and factory buildings; and so on and on. All this production transformation leading to the shiny new car would take place in mines, steel mills, small-parts subcontractor shops, assembly plants, railroads and trucking firms, advertising and marketing agencies, and finally the retail automobile dealer's show room itself, where the car is readied for sale and finally sold in the next transformation.

The TRANSFER-OR-EXCHANGE TRANSFORMATION, like the proprietary transformation, is a change in ownership only and not a real change of substance. Again this fact is symbolized by a broken-lined arrow. However, there is an important difference. Proprietary transformation refers to the change that takes place when something that is not owned or recognized as having economic value at all is finally recognized and claimed. This kind of transformation may require competitive challenge and the exercise of some kind of threat to make the claim stick. The transfer-or-exchange transformation, on the contrary, is a change from one ownership to another. It too may require some kind of threat, but it can also be completely voluntary and cooperative for all parties involved. This transformation can take place anywhere in the economic sequence from the stage of owned resources to the stage of consumer satisfactions, but it is most often thought of as a transformation in which the finished goods and services change hands from the producer to the consumer.

Unlike the other transformations, the transfer-or-exchange transformation is not always necessary. The producer is often his own consumer. We create a great variety of satisfactions for ourselves every day, acting as our own butlers, maids, cooks, chauffeurs, entertainers, home repairers, and so on. Even in the advanced economies that have become very commercialized and specialized, there is still a great deal of opportunity, not to mention need, for people to be "do-it-yourselfers". Certainly it seems that the only place to get a decent hamburger today is in your own kitchen.

When ownership does change hands, in the transfer-or-exchange transformation, the part of the transformation that is usually singled out for special attention by economists is the *exchange* part (not separately distinguishable in the diagram), which refers to those buying and selling exchanges that take place in the organized context of a store, an auction, a stock exchange, a catalogue sales office, or any other such commercial setting. Of course, these market exchanges are important, especially so in economies that lean towards free enterprise (to be defined in the next chapter). Yet, perhaps because market exchanges tend to be public events and open to easy scientific scrutiny, perhaps because they are expressed in the convenient language of money, conventional free enterprise economists have concentrated almost exclusively on them and have preferred to ignore nonmarket transfer forms of this transformation. We cannot afford such near-sightedness— "market myopia" might be a descriptive catchword for it—in this book.

If we did, we would have to disregard the great majority of all intrahousehold transfers, including all the breakfasts, lunches, dinners, provisions of good shelter and clean beds, taking-out-of-garbages, mowings of lawns, and so on that make up the giving and taking on which a household is based. We would also have to disregard all the transfers—the taxes, the welfare, the police and fire protection, the enlistments in the armed services, etc.—that ebb and flow between citizens and their governments. We would have to disregard all the charitable grants and malicious threats that are the two opposite sides of the coin of interpersonal interference. And in the more primitive societies, with economies based on foraging, noncommercial hunting and fishing, or peasant agriculture, the producer and consumer are typically one and the same household or clan, so that even less market exchange is necessary. Giving and taking effect almost all the necessary transfers of ownership here.

Surely all these nonmarket transfers, which must constitute well over half of the entire transformation, should share in the attention conventionally given to market exchanges. As you will see in Chapter Five, they do.

The CONSUMPTION TRANSFORMATION changes the finished consumer goods and services into physical and psychic satisfactions. Like the production transformation, the consumption transformation also alters the real materials and energies of the environment, and thus in many ways is a destructive process. We eat the food, we burn the fuel oil, and our automobiles are finally driven "into the ground". Nourishment, warmth, and transportation are the sources of our satisfaction in these examples; the food, the oil, and the car are our sacrificial offerings.

Not all of our economic satisfactions are so destructive. For example, the various joys of ownership—of owning art objects, a fine home, or even a good education and a healthy body—are not predicated on the gradual depletion of these commodities. In fact, some of these commodities, like a piano that must be played to keep it sounding good, appear to be enhanced through regular use. But as a general rule, we can say that the consumption transformation tends to deplete the goods and services on which it is based. In this sense, the consumption transformation and the ownership of wealth are mutually exclusive. Either we consume something or we own it; we "can't have our cake and eat it too." And since the purpose of the economic process is the satisfaction we derive from it, there would seem to be no point in accumulating anything.

But, of course, economic accumulations *do* increase our ultimate satisfaction in two ways: they provide for a "rainy day", and they can make the production transformation more efficient. The first is easiest to understand. All of us need a stocked up supply of economic goods and services to see us across those smaller and larger gaps when we are not producing. These gaps may be daily events, such as the night time, during which we are sustained in our sleep by the materials and potential energies we have accumulated in our bodies during the day. Or they may be larger gaps, such as week-ends, vacation periods, or periods of sickness or unemployment.

The second way in which accumulations increase our total satisfaction—making the production transformation more efficient—assumes at the outset that the accumulations are not in the form of consumer goods and services, but are premeditated accumulations of such things as machinery, buildings, improved agricultural land, and technology. We accumulate these things, things that we will never be able to eat or to consume in the usual sense with any satisfaction at all, for the express purpose of making our production transformation more productive. They are our tools. And if we have any foresight, we can see that denying ourselves some of the satisfactions of consumption now, in order to accumulate these tools and improve our productivity, will increase our total satisfactions in the long run.

Satisfaction, as I have said before, is what the economic process is all about. Yet, when we finally arrive at the satisfactions created by the consumption transformation, we cannot rest. These satisfactions are derived from the same human substance and the human energy that we use to drive the economic process, to make the transformations do their transforming. We apply our substance and energy to the specific transformations in such forms as legal efforts to make and hold proprietary claims, as the honest sweat and toil of productive activity, as managerial responsibility and commitment, as the organizing and operating efforts required for transfers and exchange of ownership, and as the sweet work of consuming finished products. And, when we apply our substance and energy in these ways, they are depleted.

Whether these drains represent a total undermining of

our desired economic satisfactions or not depends on how efficient our economic process is. An inefficient process can leave us thoroughly depleted, day after exhausting day. A more efficient one will enable us to build and maintain a better sense of well-being and satisfaction. Of course, we can argue that the nourishment and rest we need to face another working day are no less soul satisfying because they are needed for a working day. After all, our work may be our greatest pleasure, and the whole process leaves us more and more enriched, day after day. Objectively seen, however, it seems likely that the harder we have to work just to keep ourselves going, the less satisfaction there will be in life. That is, the greater the amount of substance and energy we must expend to fuel the economic process, the less will be left over for enjoying the "finer things of life", whatever they may be.

A final caution before we go on: Figure B is still a gross simplification—an abstraction from economic reality. No complete diagramatic layout of our economy would fit on one page or even a thousand pages of a book. Just imagine the many real-life details left out! In any one of the billions of different sequences from beginning resources to consumer satisfactions—like in the above mentioned sequence from iron ore to finished automobile—untold numbers of trans-formations of ownership, labor, materials, semifinished goods, services, and so on may take place before the finished commodity enters the consumption transformation. We certainly cannot diagram all of them here. Indeed, Figure B, as complex as it is, makes no mention of government, foreign trade, or even of money.

The primary purpose of this inquiry, then, is not to fill in all the details and draw a complete blueprint of a specific economy at a specific point in time, but rather to establish a useful format for any economy at any time. It is my fondest hope that, in this way, it will provide a sturdy new foundation on which fresh inquiries and insights can be built, come what may in our economic future.

CHAPTER 2

Ideology

Who Owns What?

Ideologically, the most important transformation in the economic sequence is the proprietary transformation. Here we find the answer to the questions: Who owns what in the world? For whose benefit does the economic process operate? When all the debts are paid off, who gets what is left over?

The vast majority of all living organisms simply claim the resources they need, and *only* those they need, from the environment, by right of their strength to do so. The roots of a tree will split a rock in their search for water; a virus will invade a living cell; foxes steal chickens; rabbits overrun New Zealand; and humanity lays claim to practically all it surveys. But tree roots will not search for petroleum; nor will viruses invade steel beams, foxes steal baseballs, or rabbits overrun the North Pole. The reason is they cannot use these things; they don't need these things; or, putting it most accurately, the benefits they can expect to get from these things would not justify the costs—the time, effort, and material—required to establish and to defend a proprietary claim over these things.

This is the main discipline of the proprietary transformation (indeed, of *all* transformations, as we shall see): the economic benefits must justify the economic costs. But this is the only justification of which we can be certain in this analysis. Personal justice, social justice, even legal, political, or military justice build on systems of ethics that are only partially—if at all—based on economic rationale. We may be tempted to insist that tree roots have an ethical right to water, but our economic sense of proprietary righteousness on behalf of these organisms is diluted to the degree that the fox finds his chickens in our hen house, that we are fighting off rabbits on our own New Zealand farm, or that the living cell that is being invaded by the above mentioned virus happens to be in our own gastrointestinal tract. In the limited economic context, most economists share with biologists the Darwinian understanding that only those organisms that are capable of pressing their claim successfully are fit enough to survive, and only those that succeed abundantly grow well and multiply. This is the usual outcome when we follow the discipline that the benefits must justify the costs. But we should not extend this simplistically to mean that the end always justifies the means or, God forbid, that might makes right.

Free Enterprise Versus Collectivism.

We may agree to hold the truth self evident "that all men [all people] are created equal;" and under rare, happy circumstances may even live by this truth, but most of us would also agree that all people are not equally endowed in all things. We would be blind to reality not to recognize that some individuals or groups of individuals generally lay claim to more of the environment than others.

When this claim becomes the expected state of affairs, when it becomes "situation normal", it becomes formalized and recognized. Recognition can elevate the claim's status to the level of an accepted economic institution, and it is sometimes even justified by an ideology. Thus, feudal monarchs in medieval Europe liked to claim their entire kingdoms, including all the people, animals, and crops therein, as personal property. When they were powerful enough to do so, they claimed usufructuary rights by taxing their subjects and impressing them into military duty, all of which was sanctioned by code and custom, by a sense of its being "natural law", and by the powerful church. In our more enlightened times (?), we prefer to temper such broad proprietary claims by some form of civil rights. By now, virtually every nation in the world at least professes some statement about the "unalienable rights" of every man (and occasionally of every woman) to "Life, Liberty and the pursuit of Happiness," regardless of how the proprietary transformation really operates in that country. All-powerful kings and queens are no longer considered acceptable in most of the modern nations today.

Two distinctly different ideologies have developed in the process of articulating and applying this more universal franchise in recent centuries. The first of these to develop, the *free enterprise system*, still permits differences in proprietary claims on the environment as long as these claims are made without resort to fraud, conspiracy, physical threat, or any other infringement of the civil rights of any other individual. That is, people may still be rich or poor, but their condition must be the result of open, legal, and ethical activities within the economic process, including the process of transferring property by inheritance. In fact, except for the limits set by this code of civil rights, the free enterprise ideology says very little about what may or may not, should or should not be done in the economic process. Its philosophy is the fewer rules and regulations, the better. Let every individual's enlightened self interest lead him to take the best opportunity of the environment, to increase his production and efficiency, and, thus, as if guided by an "invisible hand", to lead society as a whole to its optimum economic health and wealth. A harmony of interest between the individual and society is assumed, and this interest is thought to be best cultivated by freedom and free enterprise.

Actually, a truly free enterprise economy has never existed, because fraud, conspiracy, monopoly, secrecy, governmental intervention and favoritism, and other imperfections seem to stick to the human race like barnacles to barges.

The system has often functioned well, in spite of these imperfections, but, at its worst, this imperfect system can lead to glaring inequalities in the proprietary claims on the economic environment. In these instances, the free enterprise economies appear to run on the rules of the jungle, which are very little tempered by the niceties of the gentlemanly codes of civil rights and ethics.

Largely in response to this, another type of ideology, which we shall call collectivism, grew up. These anti-free enterprise ideologies, including the various forms of socialism and Marxist-Leninist or Maoist communism, differ greatly in the specifics of their origin, theory, and practice. But many of the differences are essentially political rather than economic. What all these anti-free enterprise ideologies seem to share, especially when first put into practice, is the replacement of individual autonomy with a collectivization of economic activities. That is, the remedy they prescribe for the malfunctioning of free enterprise is to wipe the slate clean of inequalities. They would expropriate and disinherit the rich and almost rich . . . and sometimes the not so rich and even the almost poor. Individual claims on land, natural resources, and on productive accumulations, such as factories and farms, are denied, and these properties are henceforth administered in the name of the entire collective constituency of the economy: "the people".

Needless to say, total collectivization has never been achieved either. It is possible to erase some of the inequalities of ownership by collectivizing land and factories. But the main flaw in the scheme is that it is highly impractical to attempt to collectivize personal resources, such as talent and intelligence, skills, wisdom, motivation and drive, or personal stature from whatever source. Just as pretty faces cannot be "government issue", collectivization just does not seem a relevant concept here.

Yet these stubbornly individual proprietary claims are not only in themselves the source of great ownership inequalities, but also a powerful instrument for *perpetuating* unequal claims on the other parts of the environment that would otherwise be amenable to egalitarian collectivization.

Even ruthlessly totalitarian collectivist economies have found that these individual differences always threaten to become the bases for the development of elites, whose preferential proprietary claims spell the failure of the collectivization itself.

In fact, the real world must make do with less-than-perfect collectivism and less-than-perfect free enterprise. Ideological realism, like politics, is the "art of the possible". The institutional structure of every economy is a trade-off between the individual dynamism and freedom possible with free enterprise, on the one hand, and the economic equality possible through collectivization, on the other. Or, to put it more negatively, it is a trade-off between the excessive proprietary claims allowed by free enterprise and the excessive subjugation of the individual required by collectivism. In our noisy and overheated ideological world, with all its conflicting social, political, cultural, and philosophical pieties, the centrality of this basic economic trade-off is often lost in the uproar.

According to conventional wisdom and practice, the government is the main force of collectivization. In modern nations, its regulations and prohibitions, its taxes and subsidies, and its outright participation in economic activity are usually in the name of the collective and are often egalitarian in intent. Even in modern economies that emphasize free enterprise, most góvernments impose some progressive taxes and operate welfare programs that redistribute some income from the rich to the poor. Some of these governments do much more. In largely collectivized economies, of course, the government gets deeply involved and often tries to plan and administer the entire economic process, right down to the monthly production and distribution of shoelaces and peppercorns. Again we have to recognize, though, that governments in both free enterprise and collectivist economies are subject to the special pleadings of particular individuals or groups and that they can be used ("abused" might be the better word) to increase the inequality of proprietary claims. Nevertheless, many of these governments remain basically egalitarian in philosophy.

Sheer size can be a powerful massifying force. That is, the subtle nuances that distinguish one individual from another are easily obliterated by the blindly aggregating and homogenizing conventions that must be adopted by institutions that become very large. Even the most sensitive big city hospital, major state university, or national army inevitably tends to evade the individuality of its constituents simply through the weight of numbers. Even basically free enterprise economies are not immune. Our individual identities may not yet have been completely reduced to our Social Security numbers, but the growing rebellious temptation to "fold, spindle, or mutilate" an important computer card occasionally on purpose, just to regain some lost individual identity, no longer seems entirely insane. And the governments are not the only massive entities: large industries and unions, mass-produced consumer goods and services, and the coinciding increase in urbanization may have an even stronger effect. While rolling along together in similar automobiles on an interstate highway, conforming our driving behavior carefully to the flow of traffic, listening to the same commercial music and talk on our radios, planning to stop at almost identical franchise restaurants and motels, going on our way to places whose customs and people are becoming more and more like those from where we came, we may ponder about our individuality. How might even a King Farouk, a St. Francis of Assisi, or a Dame Edith Sitwell have remained unique in a world such as this?

But such massification must not be confused with collectivization although they may flow from the same socioeconomic wellspring. The former is an unintentional and often lamented by-product of size. The latter is an effect produced on purpose, often achieved through size. The qualitative difference this makes in our lives is a central issue in the ideological controversy over free enterprise and collectivism. We might say it is the difference between being a fly among thousands in a barnyard and being a bee among thousands in a swarm. The difference is considered to be more than just numbers.

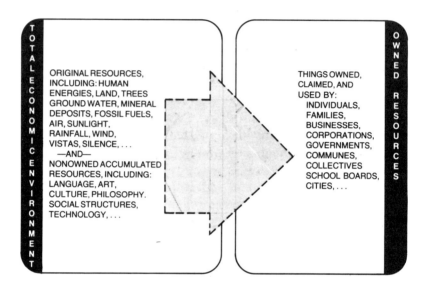

Figure C: The Proprietary Transformation

The Free Goods and Environmental Pollution.

In spite of the ideological intensity pervading the proprietary transformation, a very substantial amount of the environment is used without any formal establishment of ownership. The so-called free goods, traditionally including sunlight, rainfall, air, the oceans, large rivers and lakes, and accoustical and visual space, at least in most Western societies, have not been subject to explicit proprietary transformations at all. In earlier times, there was such an abundance of these goods that ownership of them did not have to be claimed and defended, nor could one person deprive another of the free use of them under normal circumstances. "The best things in life are free" went the song, and people were secure in the faith that the silvery moon, the smell of a pine forest on a hot afternoon, the purple mountains' majesty, the shining seas, and so on were all their birthright. Today, as growing population and increasing production presses on these resources, we can no longer be so sure about this. But the catch, as we shall see, is that the legal and ideological framework—in both free enterprise and collectivist economies—generally ignores this increasing scarcity, and continues to define them as free goods.

Obviously, the importance of these free goods to the life process and to production can hardly be overestimated. For example, losing the free air to breathe is fatal. Yet, using the free air lavishly as a dump for industrial wastes is a great way to hold down production costs. And so we have a tough dilemma on our hands: breathe or produce inexpensively. Perhaps because we live in a world where the production of goods and services for a hungry and needy global populace has been and still is the primary concern we have generally gone ahead and made lavish use of the free goods wherever possible, even in parts of the world where the populace is no longer hungry or especially needy. The result, predictably and by experience, has been the progressive pollution and depletion of the free goods in many vital areas of our environment.

As long as we think of these important resources as being free, the established patterns of environmental misuse will continue, and it will be impossible to determine what the "fittest" uses of these goods might be. In contrast, if we could somehow arrange to have these resources become owned by those who value them most through an explicit proprietary transformation, we would encourage the best and least wasteful use of this environment. For example, if airspace could be owned like real estate, I could proceed against trespassers who would like to use my air as a free dump for their industrial or automotive exhaust gases and noise. I could deny them use of it entirely, or, more likely, I could negotiate a tariff for dumping that would tend to restrict the amount dumped and also compensate me for the use of my airspace.

Of course, the added expense of having to buy or rent my dumping ground for wastes will raise the "dollar" cost of the goods and services produced by those trespassers. But it would not raise their real cost. All it would do is shift the real cost of the pollution from me, its involuntary recipient when the pollutant was freely dumped into my air, to the consumer, who must now pay me compensation via the higher price of his purchases.

If this strategy is applied uniformly throughout the economy, the ultimate consumer will pay the full real cost of the goods and services consumed. This will help the consumer weigh the decision more accurately between how much consumption he wants and how much environment he is willing to alter. He will no longer be compromised, as we all are today, by the erroneous pricing of goods and services. Today we may deplore the environmental pollution all around us, but we are nevertheless tempted into higher levels of consumption—and therefore higher levels of pollution— by the prices of goods and services that are artificially lowered by liberal use of the free goods.

Individual ownership rights over some of the formerly free goods, such as some types of airspace rights and rights to a vista, are not unheard of. The courts of many nations will be kept busy in the next decades establishing the rights and legal formats of these ownership claims. Generally, however, the civil law lags far behind the economic need, and it must seem as preposterous to the berobed guardians of our jurisprudence that anyone should want to own sunlight, rainfall, or air as it did to the American Indians when the first European settlers wanted to own land.

A more common remedy for the misuse of the environment, both in basically free enterprise economies and in collectivist ones, is to impose an explicit proprietary claim in the name of the collective, in short, to bring in the government. The formerly free goods can then be subjected to some form of management, which usually either prohibits their use entirely or establishes a body of rules and regulations governing their use. Governmental agencies that perform these functions are proliferating today in most advanced economies, some of them springing up rather hastily after real and imagined ecological disasters, like violets after a

Spring thaw. Their most useful function economically is to calculate the real costs of using the environment (which may be virtually infinite in some cases) and charge these costs to the users. For the reasons already given in connection with private ownership of formerly free goods, such user tariffs will allow the most accurate trade-off between ultimate consumption and environmental alteration.

The main advantages of collective rather than individual proprietary claims over the once free goods are that they usually carry an egalitarian intent, that they seem more directly enforced by the power of the government, and that they are not subject to the developmental lag of the civil law. For example, establishing a National Park or National Seashore in an area whose particular natural beauty is being threatened by private development instantly claims this area equally for all citizens, present and future. The main disadvantages are that, as always, collectivism has the potential to lapse into rigid dogma and inflexible obsolescence, to suppress individual freedom and dynamism, and that, to the degree that collective actions concentrate the making of large decisions in too few hands, it can commit some serious blunders (which may be saying the same thing in different ways.)

Once again we are confronted with a choice between collective and free enterprise tactics, an ideological choice that is heavily loaded with noneconomic concerns. Let us note that, on the one hand, the loss of individual dynamism in environmental issues may be especially costly. Individual dynamism, with the organic change that it causes, is the substance from which social learning and social evolution is obtained. In our world's very rapidly changing physical environment—accelerated even further by our own industrial and agricultural development— equally rapid social evolution is required if the human race is going to survive. On the other hand, while waiting for these evolutionary developments to take place, pollution increases and resources become depleted. Forceful government intervention may be needed. Before you make your ideological choice, read on all the way through Chapter Eight.

Talent, Inheritance, Land, and the Theory of Economic Rent.

We have seen that the proprietary transformation not only allows the resources of the environment to be claimed, but also it allocates them among their fittest uses through the discipline of the costs measured against the benefits of these claims. We have also seen that when part of the environment is available as free goods, the environment may be misallocated for lack of a formal proprietary transformation. The converse also exists. When part of the environment is formally and properly owned, but the claim and defense of this ownership has not and does not incur any significant real costs to the owner, then the benefits derived from this ownership are unjustified by the economic rationale of a true proprietary transformation. These unearned benefits are called *economic rent*.* As you can imagine, economic rent—like anything for free—has been a controversial issue. There is always somebody who would prefer it to flow a little more his way.

The personal environment with which we are all endowed at birth is a main source of economic rent. If we are born bright, talented, vigorous, well loved, and wealthy, our individual productive and income-earning potential will certainly look good. Yet there is no way that we can claim such gifts if we do not already have them. We can choose neither our parents nor our country of origin. And there is no need to defend our ownership of these gifts, because—although they can be squandered—they cannot be taken away. Under normal circumstances, their supply is fixed and irrevocable . . . and completely unjustified.

If such endowments at birth are significantly unequal, the unequal individual lives generated by these endowments would tend to persist even under the most egalitarian circumstances. And then it would certainly seem that "To them

---

*Economic rent differs from ordinary rent in that it refers *only* to unearned benefits and income received as a result of owning a property that just happens to be especially productive, such as the naturally photogenic face of a fashion model or farm land underneath which an oil deposit is discovered.

that has, is given." The names of the rich nations and the great families whose fortunes persist over many generations in this way are well known around the world. What they share is the concern that their original endowments not be dispersed, diluted, or exhausted, so that their next generation can again be as well endowed. That this favored next generation receives this endowment without having earned it or justified it in any way is often applauded as one of the most important and positive forces for national and personal responsibility, dynamism, and efficiency. Providing for our children is considered the bedrock of good citizenship.

The fact remains, however, that inheritance income is an unearned economic rent and—at least, in the case of personal inheritance—is therefore anathema to an intensely egalitarian ideology. Even mildly collectivist economies typically restrict the range of possible inheritance, especially the inheritance of material accumulations, such as real estate and securities. Eventually a family's summer castle and gardens must be sold off to the state to pay for the delinquent inheritance taxes. Restrictions, however, are less possible with the intangible forms of inheritance, such as cultural values, genetic endowments, and family connections. A good upbringing, a love of learning, and the appreciation of good friends can be passed on from generation to generation, but they cannot be taxed.

In the end, it is a question of ideology. The aggregate payoff from the individual freedom and economic dynamism of a liberal inheritance policy must be weighed against the collectivist virtues of the economic equality to be obtained through a restrictive inheritance policy. In either case, reality necessitates a compromise. We have seen that some inheritance is possible even in intensely egalitarian economies. Conversely, even in intensely free enterprise economies, inheritance is hardly absolute. Profligate sons and dissolute daughters will see to that. Furthermore, public education is purposely designed to soften the inequalities of cultural and educational heritage among families, and material inheritances are usually taxed anyway, if not for purposes of collective equality than merely for government revenue.

One of the main sources of economic rent (and the original definition of the term) is the unearned income produced from land ownership. Like other proprietary claims, land is originally claimed or purchased for a real cost that may not exceed the benefits to be derived from it. But unlike many other accumulations of ownership, land (if not its fertility) endures practically forever and is in practically fixed supply. Given a well-ordered and well-enforced real estate law, the only cost of claiming and defending this ownership, except for taxes, will be the original cost of the land. And given a growing population with a growing need for food and all the other products of the land, the benefits to be derived from the original piece of land will increase. To put it precisely, as land becomes relatively more scarce, the valuations of its product will increase. These new increases, however, are unearned income for the landowner, because no additional costs in either energy or materials were incurred. The new income is strictly an accident of the growing population seeking support more and more intensively from a fixed area of land. Thus, an increasing proportion of the landlord's income may be called economic rent.*

As a whole, economic rent may seem unfair. Whether it is an endowment at birth, a family affair, or an accident of history, it is, after all, something for nothing. But it does have the effect of making a lot of us strive to be the first to claim a resource in the environment, to "get while the getting is good!" Economist John Stuart Mill (1806-1873) deplored this greedy "trampling, crushing, elbowing, and treading on each other's heels", but admitted that it seemed to be a phase of progress. Perhaps its virtue is that it keeps us lively.

Theft, Collusion, and Discrimination.

One of the time-honored threats against proprietary claims is theft. We need say little here about criminal theft, although

---

*We are dealing with *land* landlords here. In common usage, the term landlord seems to apply not so much to owners of original land as to the owners of buildings. Depending on whether or not it was unearned, the "rent" these building-landlords receive may or may not be real economic rent.

the economics of crime is an important branch of the science. (A short, very basic analysis of it will be introduced in Chapter Five.) Most thieves, from pickpockets to embezzlers, probably have strong noneconomic motives as well as economic ones, but the economic content of their actions is glaringly obvious. This is not always true of noncriminal theft.

One important form of noncriminal theft is the abduction of a proprietary claim without the owner's awareness and sometimes even without the abductor's awareness. For example, insecticides and herbicides do the job for which they are intended at a cost to us consisting of their purchase price and application costs. These costs are expected. But some of the chemical compounds employed have been found to incur unexpected hidden costs through the deterioration of the health of our land, trees and plants, domestic animals, and even of ourselves. Unlike the abuse of free goods, this kind of abuse is imposed on already claimed and owned resources. In effect, it is a theft from us, because it is perpetrated by the producers, albeit sometimes innocently at first, with the object of continuing an economic activity that is beneficial to themselves. If there were no such objective, the abuse would be recognized as an unfortunate accident and would be stopped forthwith. But *with* this objective, the producers might be hesitant to quit. In fact, these thefts can become blatant and recurring, at which point they may have to be formally redefined as criminal acts through the creation of new laws and regulations. Outlawing various food colorings and additives, thalidomide, and D.D.T. was not the beginning, nor will it be the end. As the products of our economy become technologically more abstruse, the opportunity for this kind of theft—and the consequent list of formal bans—will grow.

Another form of theft is made possible by collusion. What one of us may not be able to claim, because our claim is not powerful enough, may be successfully claimed by a conspiracy of similarly motivated individuals. Of course, when group action is openly and successfully practiced by such organizations as political parties, consumer groups, and civil rights groups, it is not called theft; it is called team effort. I suppose the ethical objectives of these groups justify their means, and they can be important engines of social justice. When such team effort is practiced by producers' lobbies and associations or labor unions, the objectives are often less easily legitimated. And when these means are applied to unethical objectives, as is done by hoodlum and racketeer gangs, the fruits of such collusion can only be called theft.

Different times and different ideologies draw the line differently between what is considered a justifiable or even a noble team effort and what is considered a criminal conspiracy. It is probably character building to be concerned about the ethical distinction between what is and what is not theft through collusion. Our economic analysis clearly shows, however, that collusion for economic advantage is always a shifting of proprietary claims from the previous owner to the colluding group, whose members could not make these claims successfully as individual actors. Like it or not, it is a mob action.

Neither free enterprise ideology nor collectivist ideology welcomes collusion. Free enterprise deplores the way collusion undermines individualism and attacks collusion not only with the doctrine of criminal conspiracy but also with various antitrust laws, laws restricting labor unions and special interest lobbies, and a general readyness to consider suspending the rights of assembly in instances of strikes, demonstrations, and other group displays. Collectivism recognizes in collusion a more cardinal sin: the usurpation of its own identity. Unless the labor unions, political parties, trusts and cartels, or other collusive groups have been co-opted by the ruling collective itself, the more totalitarian the collective is, the more likely the colluding groups will be strictly outlawed from the start. Thus, communists today do not tolerate political opposition parties or independent labor unions at all, and even milder collectivists, such as democratic socialists, may look askance at private cooperatives or mutual aid societies. Yet collusion survives.

Similar to collusion is the implicit theft that is both the

economic purpose and the economic result of discrimination. For example, denying people opportunities for employment, education, or housing, or any other proprietary claims, on the basis of their race, sex, or age is denying them access to parts of the environment to which they otherwise may have made the fittest claim. Whatever you or I may think about the morality or the ideology of such a policy, the effect, at first glance, would seem to be that discrimination makes more environmental resources available to the discriminators at the expense of those discriminated against, which has the same effect as outright theft. And, since successful theft benefits the thief, discrimination pays off. However, one of the most valuable components of the environment available to each of us is the creativity and productivity of others in our society. People are our most important resource. And since discrimination inhibits the full creativity and productivity of the people who are discriminated against, it steals not only from them but from the discriminators also.

Ending discrimination, then, not only results in a great improvement in the potential proprietary claims of the offended groups; it can also result in a substantial net increase in the proprietary potential of the former discriminators. Although this is small comfort to those whites, for example, who may feel their economic status threatened by the competition from the newly integrated blacks in their schools, neighborhoods, and jobs, it is the only purely economic rationale for ending this racial discrimination. In the long run, it is an amply sufficient rationale. Unhappily, people also have to live in the short run, and that is what all the conflict is about.

CHAPTER 3

Making Decisions

Production and Consumption.

For all the importance of the proprietary transformation, the physical world remains mostly unchanged by it. Again, its arrow is drawn with broken lines in Figures B and C for this reason. The only real change wrought on the physical world by the economic system takes place in the production and the consumption transformations.

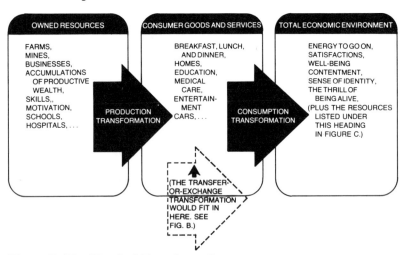

Figure D: The Physical Transformations

In the production transformation, we make finished consumer goods and services out of both the free and the claimed—but as yet raw—resources of the environment. This is the most conspicuous, tangible, physical sort of transformation. It is variously a noisy, sweaty, exciting, inspiring, tedious, boring, and grinding drama that plays not only in our factories, shipyards, highways, farms, mines, forests, and shopping centers, but also in our homes, churches, government offices, clubs, vacation resorts, and military camps. Anywhere and anytime that physical materials and energies are moved closer to the point where they may be consumed, the production transformation commands the stage. Its theater is our entire landscape—the plains and mountains, the waters, the sky—which seems to change under our very eyes as a result.

Production is so emphatically an economic process that it has often come to be seen as the economic process. After all, in a hungry world, the problem has always been insufficient production, and national economic development is defined as increased production. For centuries economists searched the production transformation for the fountain of economic creativity; the source of value. For some, the productivity of land, of "Mother Earth", was the wellspring. Others saw the hand of God kindling the productive powers. And human labor, accumulations of capital, the driving entrepreneurial spirit, or combinations of all these and more have also come in for their share of the credit. But always the origins of economic creation were (and usually still are) seen as dwelling in the production transformation.

Occasionally distribution shares the spotlight with production. Ideological issues usually focus more on the distributive process than the productive one. That is, a steel mill works about the same way in the Soviet Union as it does in the United States; what is different is the way these two economies distribute the ownership and the products of this mill. For the same reason, economic reforms, including tax reforms and welfare measures, often concentrate their attack on the distribution of income and wealth, regarding the production of these either as given, as desirable in any case, or as just plain irrelevant to the problem. Yet even this seems to reaffirm the primacy—the inevitability—of production more than deny it.

The production emphasis is more easily understood than justified. Just as we cannot single out the motor, the drive train, or the wheels as the part of the automobile that creates the forward motion, so we cannot single out one transformation as the creator or even the *primus inter pares* of creators of economic value. Each transformation is null and void without its neighbors, and, with the occasional exception of the transfer-or-exchange transformation, all are required in the economic sequence. Furthermore, production is not the only physical transformation of tangible materials and energies in the economic sequence. That scene is shared by the consumption transformation.

The consumption transformation takes the finished goods and services and creates our physical and psychic economic satisfactions with them. Our houses and apartments become our satisfaction at being sheltered and secure; breakfasts, lunches, and dinners become the pleasure of eating and the contentment of being well fed; an evening at the opera or at a jazz concert becomes the sense of enrichment gained from art and beauty; and so on. That consumption often takes place more privately in homes and families, often by ourselves or among friends, makes it less conspicuous, perhaps, than the production transformation. But consumption is just as physical a transformation as production. What the consumer products become, what the houses and the breakfasts and the operas turn into, is our own psychic satisfaction, our physical growth and health, and our will to go on. This is certainly as impressive a physical transformation as production, at its most dramatic, can achieve.

And consumption is not always so quiet. Some of us delight in a conspicuous display of our consumption activity by making a show of the clothes we wear, the diet we eat, the housing we live in, and the schools, hospitals, theaters, automobiles, resort hotels, and entertainments we use. All of us, intentionally or not, attest to our level of consumption by the state of our mental and physical health, our vigor, and our material standard of living.

Aggregating everyone's level of consumer well-being for one year into a single statistical sum would give us a "Gross National Satisfaction" figure that would be the best and most interesting indicator of our economy's success at this kind of achievement. However, being psychic states, different people's satisfactions are hard enough to enumerate and harder yet to add together. "What's one man's poison is another's meat." So, perhaps, we could settle for a "Gross National Consumer Goods and Services", which would aggregate the actual and estimated dollar values of all the goods and services entering consumption transformations in one year. This would include the estimated dollar values of the consumer goods and services produced in the home, as well as the actual dollar values of those bought in the market. Dollars are always a convenient, if often a misleading, common denominator. This statistic would certainly be possible to obtain with the present state of statistical and data processing technology, but no nation does so at present. Instead, the best accounting available is an aggregate statistic of only those consumer goods and services entering the consumption transformation by being purchased with money in one year. It is called, as we might expect by now, not Gross National Consumer Goods and Services, but Gross National Product.

Economic productivity, the creation of value, the level of consumption, the Gross National Product, and the material standard of living do interest economists. But the actual performance of production and consumption activity does not. This is more likely to be the concern of engineers, managers, agriculturalists, designers and architects, dieticians, home economists, and the like. The prime concern of economics is the *cybernetics* of production and consumption, that is, the decision making that guides these transformations. In this respect, we will see that the economic analyses of the production and consumption transformations are so similar that they can be described and analyzed simultaneously. Furthermore this analysis applies equally well in either free enterprise or collectively oriented economies, or, for that matter, to the production and consumption behavior of little green people on Mars, should such people exist.

In fact, production and consumption are often inseparably combined in one act. For example, when we enjoy an afternoon hike through the country, we are producing and consuming the sources of our satisfaction at the same time. The extent to which a transfer-and-exchange transformation is interposed between the production transformation and the consumption transformation (see Figure B) attests only to the specialization and commercialization attained by the economy. It does not require splitting the analysis of these transformations, and we will analyze them together here.

Proportions of Time and Space.

Distilled to the basic essentials, the ownable resources of the environment are limited by only two dimensions: time and space. That is, in the universe we occupy, our planet plus its share of solar energies is the practical reach of our economic space so far, and there are no more than twenty-four hours in every day for economic activity. These limits are fixed, at least at present. Within them, populations may expand and contract, cultures may flourish and die, ideologies may struggle for dominance, technologies may be created and destroyed, and wealth may accumulate and dissipate. But the two dimensions of our economic environment that must ultimately be economized, because they cannot be reproduced, are space—meaning physical matter and energy—and time. Of course, technological advances and the growing sophistication of the economic process will loosen the effective limits imposed by these dimensions. Indeed, that is the name of the game of economic progress: time will be used more effectively and new resources will be recognized in the environment. Nothing enhances the value of dried and wrinkled rose hips so much as suddenly discovering that they are a concentrated source of vitamin C. However, for the sake of this analysis, let us assume that technology and economic sophistication are fixed at the existing level, for the time being.

The production and consumption transformations have the primary responsibility for economizing time, energies, and materials. While production and consumption decisions usually appear to be concerned with money, labor, materials, products—all the everyday productive and finished goods and services—they are ultimately concerned with elemental time and space. What this economizing in production and consumption means is that every hour spent in one pursuit is lost to all other possible activities, every acre devoted to one kind of crop is lost to all other possible land uses, and every ton of iron ore destined for automobile steel is denied other applications. It is a question of alternatives. All alternatives must be considered, and since only one can be chosen, the best one must be chosen. Any other choice would be irrational and illogical or simply would not be a choice at all.

Unfortunately, the best alternative is not always easily identified. One reason for this difficulty is that we must make these decisions about actions yet to be taken (production and consumption transformations are actions), and this means we have to try to predict the outcome for a future time. Predicting the future, of course, is always problematical. It is often difficult enough to make little choices over short periods of time intelligently. Trying to choose the very best among the various flavors of ice-cream in an ice-cream store is difficult, because it is hard for us to predict accurately how pleasing each of the alternatives would taste. It is, of course, much more difficult to make larger decisions that concern longer periods of time, such as choosing the best career to prepare for in college or trying to decide between building a windmill or a solar powered electric generator, because it is even harder to predict how each of these alternatives would turn out.

Another reason the best alternative is not always easily identified is that the world—our economic space—will not "hold still". Production and consumption are the physical transformations in the economic process that make it entropic. Resource depletion, pollution, and environmental change accompany these transformations at every step. What seems at first to be a good alternative, for example, aerosol spray cans that make so many product applications a simple matter of pushing a button, can come to haunt us, as the chlorofluorocarbon propellants used in these cans eat away our life preserving atmospheric ozone layer.

The Futurity of Decisions.

For these reasons, economists prefer to think that we break down both the "futurity" and the extent of our production and consumption decisions into their shortest possible time and space components. They prefer to think that we deal with small marginal decisions, such as whether or not to increase or decrease the automobile production level on the assembly line we are managing by one car per hour, or whether or not to change our personal consumption of shoes by one pair per year.

Not all decision processes can be carried out in such small increments or decrements. For example, we cannot choose to have just half a baby; the smallest marginal unit in expanding family size is one whole human being. Also it used to be that we could not get married by small steps. We either took the big jump, or we did not. Times change.

Nor is behavior by small increments or decrements—called *marginaltiy,* because these changes add or subtract at the margin of our total behavior pattern—always and exclusively preferred. True heroic behavior allows no such timid and piddling adjustments; it is of a much grander design. The sweep of genius, the audacity of talent, and the compelling urge of romance are also great dynamic forces in the economy. Whether progress, biological evolution, or social learning are most often carried forward by many sequential marginal steps taken in the humdrum, everyday course of events or whether they are most often carried forward by infrequent but major chance events, genetic sports, or societal "great leaps" that fire the dramatic imagination remains a provocative and popular philosophic question. We might note, however, that even the most heroic behavior of an individual often appears safely marginal when viewed from the perspective of the larger organism in which the individual is a member. For example, the wild mutation of one polyp in a coral reef constitutes only a tiny marginal genetic change for the entire reef. Likewise, a brilliant breakthrough in metallurgical technology that revolutionizes the alloying of tungsten and steel may be only one change among many in the production processes of a large, integrated steel mill and may be a barely perceptible adjustment for the steel industry as a whole. If it fails, probably only a few technicians and lower level managers would lose their jobs.

In this sense, what is and what is not marginal becomes a relative judgment. Nevertheless, there are limits to the dimensions within which this relativity exists. To continue with the example of a metallurgical breakthrough, if the entire steel industry were collectively managed through a central administration, the industry-wide adoption of the new alloy technology may be less an incremental marginal step than an heroic leap, which, if it falls flat, could have the entire central administration's heads rolling. Powerfully centralized control, such as might be found in a large corporation or governmental administration, tends to deny marginalism its first individualistic, atomistic steps. Yet, be it large unit or small, centrally administered or individually independent, rational behavior always *tries* to be as cautiously incremental, as marginal as possible. We all prefer to test the water with our toes before jumping in. It is the only predictable kind of behavior in any kind of economy: collectivist, free enterprise, or whatever. Accordingly, it will be the only kind of decision process we will analyze here.

The Law of Eventually Diminishing Marginal Returns.

Finding the one best alternative course of action will not complete the decision, however. Even the simplest of organisms, the aforementioned polyp in the coral reef, for example, would not "decide" to do just one thing—eat or reproduce or excrete—to the exclusion of everything else, at least, not for long. It would not, and it could not, because just eating or just reproducing or just excreting would be physically impossible. Such an idiotic fixation over any longer period of time would result in a highly inefficient (a fatal) imbalance in the proportions of the various needs on which the polyp's life depends. Indeed, the definition of the best alternative turns out to be that action that best responds to the organism's most urgent needs and opportunities at the moment. Depending on the condition it is in, depending on what went on before and where it is now, any one of the polyp's relatively simple needs could be singled out as the most urgent, and any of a number of different actions could be defined as the best available alternative. If the polyp has not eaten recently, it might be hungry, and getting something to eat might be the first order of business at that particular moment.

Humans, of course, have a more complex variety of needs, opportunities, and satisfactions. For better or for worse, our available alternatives for action range much further than just eating, reproducing, and excreting, and we will have to admit that our lives are, at least, more interesting than the lives of polyps in a coral reef. But our efforts at identifying and evaluating the best alternative uses of our available time and space are governed by the same law: the law of eventually diminishing marginal returns. All this law amounts to is that as one ingredient in a mix is increased proportionately to the others, its incremental contribution to the sustenance and enhancement of the total mix will eventually diminish.

Let us consider an example that could be familiar to any of us who have ever tried our talents in the kitchen: making a cake. We know that, as eggs are added to a cake batter, they contribute to the wholesomeness of the cake, the first egg making a big contribution, the second a contribution perhaps just as big. But with the third egg in most cakes, the extra contribution is not as big. While it may still be desirable, this egg is probably not as critical to the cake's wholesomeness as the first or second. Returns per egg are beginning to diminish. The fourth egg may also still create positive returns, although they will be less than those of the third egg. And so returns will diminsh for each next egg, each egg "on the margin". Should a fiftieth (!) egg finally be added to the otherwise unchanged recipe, the batter will have become an unwholesome mess resembling misbegotten scrambled eggs more than a cake batter. Because of these diminishing returns from additional (marginal) eggs, we cannot bake a cake made only of eggs or only of flour, milk, sugar, spices, shortening, or leavening, for that matter. All ingredients are subject to the same law of eventually diminishing marginal returns.

Furthermore, we must remember that the eggs did not come free from outer space or from the Garden of Eden. The more eggs that were used in the cake, the fewer were available for alternative uses. Having to forgo these alternative uses incurs what economists call an "opportunity cost", which means literally the implicit cost of being unable to take advantage of the next best opportunity to use the egg.

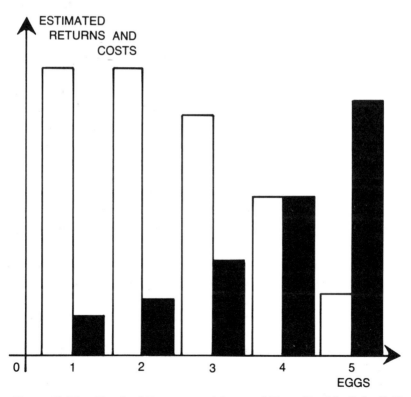

Figure E: The Marginal Returns and Costs of Eggs Used in Cake Batter

Since the alternative uses are also subject to the law of eventually diminishing marginal returns, the increasing number of eggs used in the cake batter means that eggs are denied to more and more essential uses, and the opportunity cost for each successive egg rises. That is, the first few eggs in the cake may have been alternatively used for an egg shampoo, as a supplement to the dog's food, or in some other nonessential use. But, unless the supply of eggs is free and unlimited, the next eggs—let us say the fourth and fifth— used in the cake may have to be those that would have been otherwise used for breakfast. And the fiftieth egg in cake batter may mean starving the baby half to death!

A graph shows these relationships between the number of eggs used and each egg's estimated returns (contribution to the wholesomeness of the cake) and its estimated costs (alternative use of the egg that must be foregone) particularly well. Estimated returns and costs are measured vertically on the graph; eggs are enumerated horizontally. The white bars indicate returns per egg; the black bars indicate costs.

Notice that by the time we reach egg number four, the costs are estimated to be equal to the returns. This is the optimum point that maximizes the *net* returns (total returns from all the eggs used minus total costs of all the eggs used) from using eggs in the cake. If we mistakenly put in a fifth egg, it costs more than it is worth. If we mistakenly stop adding eggs before we reach egg number four, we cannot be sure that we have chosen the best alternative use for our eggs, because the returns of eggs in the cake still exceed the returns of eggs in their alternative uses (indicated by the costs of eggs).

Conveniently, this example applies both to a production decision and to a consumption decision, depending on whether we think of ourselves as using the eggs to produce a cake or as consuming eggs via the cake. In my kitchen, there is not much difference between these points of view.

Thus, to sum up what we have analyzed so far, economic production and consumption behavior is a matter of finding and evaluating the best alternatives among a variety of activities that use available time and space. All of these activities are carefully adjusted by marginal increases and decreases in an effort to respond to our most urgent needs and opportunities. Each single alternative is subject to the discipline of the law of eventually diminishing marginal returns, so a mixture of alternatives is usually the most efficient, the most effective, the most successful pattern of behavior.

With such a neat solution to the decision problem, we may be tempted to believe that marginal analysis can optimize our economic behavior once and for all. But this "best mix" of alternatives, this optimum behavior achieved by careful marginal decisions still provides only the maximum net return *realistically* possible; it does not provide the absolute maximum that would completely satisfy all of our needs and desires. Unfortunately, complete bliss is still some way off. The Garden of Eden that would supply us with the unlimited materials, energies, and activity time required for such absolute maximization exists only in our dreams, if it exists at all. Furthermore, our every effort to optimize among our alternatives consumes some of the substance on which our satisfactions were based. Entropy continues its stealthy process, and the world does not hold still for permanent solutions. So sober economic reality insists that we carefully budget the ingredients of our available time and space on an ongoing basis, with the less useful ingredients always being traded off for the more useful ones, in order to achieve our daily bread in only the best of all possible worlds.

Work and Leisure.

Since our efforts to make the economy run—to drive the transformation processes—tend to deplete the very satisfactions that are the purpose of all economic activity, this activity can appear to be somewhat self-defeating. Just as we can spend so much time choosing exactly the right clothes to wear to a party that we miss most of the party, we can also work so hard and consume so much that we forget to enjoy life. Again, a trade-off is called for, this time between optimizing production and consumption efforts, and conserving and enjoying satisfactions.

The trade-off between work, on the one hand, and conserving and enjoying satisfactions—call it leisure—on the other, is one of the most basic economic decisions to be made. As such, it is itself the marginal decision that supersedes all others.* Yet, in most advanced economies, it is hardly given much attention at all. Regardless of ideology, geographic location, varying personal preferences, or any other distinguishing feature, the division of the day between work and leisure is usually taken as a *fait accompli*. Like soldiers in lockstep, most of us simply march to work from nine to five, five days a week, or whatever the local convention demands.

Reconsidering the convention collectively in unions, governments, or managements happens at most occasionally, perhaps at semiannual intervals or at "contract time". Defying the convention and following our own individual preferences for work and leisure will almost certainly get us fired, especially if we opt for more leisure and less work. Evaluating the work-leisure trade-off continuously and making ongoing marginal adjustments, like we might do with eggs in cake batter or the production rate of automobiles on an assembly line, is practically unheard of. Instead, we just march on from nine to five. Perhaps the very rich can escape this lockstep, but numerically it is mostly the world's poor, those living in unindustrialized and undeveloped economic conditions, who are free to decide daily how much to work or not to work. But what a bitter freedom it is! At its most brutal, they are free to work or to starve, *if* they can find any useful work to do.

If we were free to make our own marginal decisions

---

*Granted that we may derive many pleasures from a day's work well done, we shall nevertheless define work as an onerous effort that should be avoided if possible and only performed if properly rewarded. This reward—the positive net satisfactions derived from the goods and services produced by work—is one measure by which the optimum balance between work and leisure will be determined. The other measure is the cost of work in terms of lost leisure time.

about the best trade-off between work and leisure, here is how we would do it: We would predict the net satisfactions to be gained from work. These would consist of all the satisfactions gained from the consumer goods and services we get in exchange for our work minus all the costs—the time, energy, and other resources spent—of working for and consuming these goods and services. Surprisingly, even taken as a whole, the satisfactions derived from all consumer goods and services are subject to the law of eventually diminishing marginal returns. This is so for two reasons: one, the work to acquire these goods and services is onerous and takes time away from leisure; and two, even if the goods and services came to us for free, there is a human limit to how much we can comfortably consume. Stated simply and obviously, we do not normally have an insatiable desire for the satisfactions derived from consuming goods and services. In the end, we can only eat, drink, travel, wear, house and furnish, be entertained, and party so much.

In making the work-leisure decision, we would also predict the satisfactions that we would gain from leisure. Leisure is an end in itself, that is, it produces satisfactions directly, especially if leisure activities are imaginative and varied. But leisure activities are also subject to the law of eventually diminishing marginal returns, because: one, like work, leisure activities can also deplete some of the energies and resources created by work; two, they take time away from work and its rewards; and three, what may be saying the same thing, we do not normally have an insatiable desire for leisure. There is a point when rest and relaxation may seem more like boredom and unemployment.

The point to predicting the satisfactions to be derived from work and leisure is that we can then compare the different levels of satisfactions derived from different amounts of work and leisure. The trade-off procedure is then the same as the one used to allocate eggs between a cake and their alternative uses. Now, however, we would be allocating our own time between work and leisure. This is illustrated hypothetically in Figure F below, which tells essentially the same story as Figure E, the eggs-in-the-cake example, except that a table of numbers is used instead of a bar graph. The numbers here are only meant to symbolize returns or satisfactions. Returns or satisfactions probably cannot be accurately enumerated this way, so the numbers must be taken with a grain of salt. They do illustrate the analysis accurately, though.

Hours of work	Marginal returns from this hour	Total returns from work	Hours of leisure	Marginal returns from this hour	Total returns from leisure	Grand total: returns from work and leisure
16	.40	19.40	0	0	0	19.40
15	.50	19.00	1	1.60	1.60	20.60
14	.60	18.50	2	1.60	3.20	21.70
13	.70	17.90	3	1.50	4.70	22.60
12	.80	17.20	4	1.50	6.20	23.40
11	.90	16.40	5	1.40	7.60	24.00
10	1.00	15.50	6	1.40	9.00	24.50
9	1.10	14.50	7	1.30	10.30	24.80
8	1.20	13.40	8	1.20	11.50	24.90
7	1.30	12.20	9	1.10	12.60	24.80
6	1.50	10.90	10	1.00	13.60	24.50
5	1.70	9.40	11	.90	14.50	23.90
4	1.80	7.70	12	.80	15.30	23.00
3	1.90	5.90	13	.70	16.00	21.90
2	2.00	4.00	14	.60	16.60	20.60
1	2.00	2.00	15	.50	17.10	19.10
0	0	0	16	.40	17.50	17.50

Figure F: The Work-Leisure Trade-off

Our *objective*, of course, would be to maximize total returns, that is, total satisfactions. Our *procedure*, however, would not deal directly with total returns, but would focus most pointedly once again on marginal returns, on the returns of the "next egg", so to speak. And from here on it would be just simple arithmetic. Let us suppose that there are only sixteen hours a day in which to decide between work and leisure, the other eight being preempted by sleep. And suppose furthermore, since we have to start somewhere, that we—you or I or someone else—would be devoting all sixteen hours to work. "All work and no play" is unlikely to be optimal for anyone, so we would experiment with marginally reducing our daily work time by one hour to fifteen hours in order to gain one hour of leisure. If we would discover that the net satisfactions of the goods and services we gave up by working one hour less are not as great as the satisfaction gained from the hour of leisure, then our total satisfaction returned from our sixteen hours would have increased. Thus encouraged, we would be likely to try to increase our total satisfaction even more by reducing our work day another marginal hour to fourteen hours, in order to gain a second hour of leisure.

We would continue to adjust the proportion of work to leisure until we find that the satisfactions lost from reducing work time are not less than the satisfactions gained from having more leisure. Or, to put it into economists' language, we will have maximized our total returns when the returns of the marginal (last reduced or added) hour of work *equals* the returns of the marginal hour of leisure.

Had we begun with sixteen hours devoted to leisure instead of work, the outcome would still have been the same. So much leisure is also unlikely to be optimal, and we would therefore have experimented with giving up some leisure time for work time until the satisfaction lost from a reduction of leisure was no longer less than the satisfactions gained from an increase in work. Thus we would have arrived at the same point, but from the opposite direction.

Perhaps the most important single determinant of where this optimum point will be—how the day's sixteen hours will be divided between work and leisure, is our wage rate. All of us who have ever earned an honest dollar know that the returns from work are largely determined by our wage rate. If this rate is high, the resulting high purchasing power will enable us to buy many satisfaction producing commodities; if it is low, the converse is true. So, while each hour apportioned to work or leisure is measured like any other, in terms of time, its value, in terms of the satisfactions it produces, can be widely varied. A change in the wage rate will alter the optimum proportion of work and leisure.

Economists have found that when wage rates are first increased, work becomes more desirable, because it produces greater returns. Tempted by all the satisfactions that our newly higher wage rates promise us, we gladly give up some leisure time for more work time. Our optimum proportion will then consist of more work and less leisure than at lower wage rates. This is called the *substitution effect*, because work is substituted for leisure. However, when wage rates increase even more, we begin to feel that the extra money and the extra satisfactions this money can buy is no longer of the same critical importance. We begin to feel the law of eventually diminishing marginal returns in our work hours. Meanwhile, as our work time has increased, our leisure time has decreased, and each successively lost moment of leisure is more and more painful. Whereas at first we lost the leisure time to play cards in the afternoon, now we do not even have time for a drink before dinner. So, with the very much higher wage rates, our optimum proportion will once again begin to tend towards less work and more leisure. This is called the *income effect*, because the larger income produced by the higher wages reduces our need for even more income, allows us to indulge in more leisure, and also gives us more money to spend during our leisure hours, which raises their rate of returns and makes leisure more attractive.

We certainly make these fundamental decisions about work and leisure more by intuition or "feel" than by a set of numbers like those in Figure F. As already mentioned, expressing returns or satisfactions numerically is very unrealistic. The table is merely a tool to illustrate the way in which an optimum is achieved when the marginal returns of the eighth hour of leisure. And this much, this perceived equality, is, in fact, realistic: we can tell when we have had enough of something and when we have found an optimum proportion, an optimum mix. This means that we can per- · ceive the equality of the marginal returns from work and leisure, even if we cannot put numbers on it.

Therefore, the length of the list of evaluated alternatives in Figure F, all the way from sixteen hours of work and no leisure to the extreme opposite combination, is also quite unrealistic. And it is quite unnecessary. Normally, the ongoing marginal decision process itself will assure that we are always reasonably near our optimum proportions, except under drastic circumstances. Our considered adjustments will seldom involve more than fine tuning, a marginal step up or down. The fact that our lockstep, nine to five allocation of time to work is *not* the result of such marginal fine tuning qualifies it as one of the drastic economic circumstances existing in modern economies today.

When is Enough Enough?

All this meticulous marginal analysis is a conventional and generally accepted form of economic analysis. Its logic is clear, self-evident, and hardly refutable. The overall perspective of the decision system on which this analysis is based is illustrated in Figure G below. Here the economic actor—you,

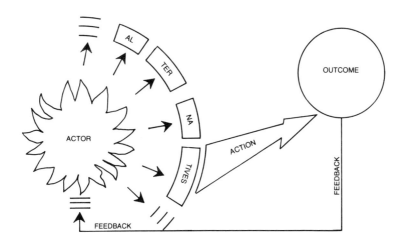

Figure G: The Decision System

I, or some other person—considers as many alternatives as are known to him and, on the basis of their predicted outcomes, chooses to act on the most promising one. The resulting outcome is signaled back to the actor via the feedback loop. If the outcome is satisfactory, the same action will be taken again when the need is felt again. If the feedback loop signals a less than satisfactory outcome, the need will not be served, and another alternative will be chosen and acted upon. Alternative actions will continue to be chosen until a satisfactory outcome is perceived.

But here is a problem: the outcome is not always accurately or completely perceived. As is indicated in the illustration, a threshold, symbolized by triple barrier lines, prevents the feedback loop from reaching the actor un-obstructed.* This threshold can be high enough that the actor cannot perceive the unsatisfactory nature of the outcome of his action, and, thus, he will be led to take the same action again and again by mistake. For example, the physical and mental problems that cause alcoholism or obesity can be analytically described as an inability to perceive the strongly diminished marginal returns that are obtained from consuming more alcohol or more snacks. In these cases, the victim seems to be driven to act again and again, to overdrink or overeat, because he is blind to the results, even as they become more and more disastrous.

Fortunately such pathological decision behavior is ab-normal in individuals, and most of us usually get our signals from the feedback loop straight sooner or later. But this pathological error is less abnormal in the economic decision behavior of larger aggregated economic actors, such as cor-porations, governments, cooperatives, communes, and the

---

*Notice, by the way, that Figure G also shows two other triple lined threshold symbols that are on either side of the al-ter-na-tives list. These indicate that we usually are not aware of all the possible alternatives we could have considered before taking an action. Of course, the more alternatives we consider, the more accurate and efficient our final choice is likely to be. Education is our telescope for spotting more and better alternatives and, as we shall see in Chapter Four, an economist's definition of education might well be "the instrument by which our life's alterna-tives are increased".

like. Communication always becomes a potential problem when a lot of people are involved. Face to face contact is lost, differences in personal preferences are blurred or misunderstood, messages get garbled and delayed, and the right hand ends up not knowing that there is a left hand, much less what the left hand is doing. When corporation presidents, government agency chiefs, and professors of management stress the value of communication as often as they do, it is a good tip-off that intraorganizational communication is usually a problem. The threshold interposed between their feedback loop and the deciding person becomes an insuperable wall of administrative offices, red tape, inertia, anonymity, irresponsibility, and a standing invitation for errors to creep into the information.

Even if intraorganization communication were as loud and clear as a mockingbird on a summer morning, the problem would not be solved. The definitive characteristic of organizations is that they are just that; organizations, purposeful aggregations of numerous individuals. And, just as the individual cells in living bodies forfeit their autonomy to the degree that their body is centrally controlled, so individual people must forfeit their autonomy in economic decision making to the degree that the organizations to which they belong—the corporations, agencies, families, communes—usurp these powers in their central control.

Organization, then, always comes at a cost to the individuals involved. The cost is the loss of their individual autonomy. Freud generalized and called this process socialization, which he found to be at the expense of the id; for our purposes it suffices to point out that, when an organization imposes its rule over individuals, the individuals are no longer able to make marginal decisions according to their own unique personal preferences. They are no longer able to find and act upon their own individual optimum proportions—where their marginal returns of personal satisfactions are perceived to be equal—in such everyday matters as hours of work and leisure, wages and work time, how they spend their money, what food they eat, how much they travel, bend over a machine, sit still or stand, and what other people they must associate with. To a fully organized, hard working family man or woman coming home in the evening on the crowded commuter train or highway, the idea of wanton, unemployed and irresponsible bachelorlike unattachedness must look very tempting at times.

When individuals are subsumed into an organization, our decision system becomes more roundabout, as illustrated in Figure H below. Now, instead of receiving the feedback directly from the outcome of our actions, the feedback is filtered through the organization. And now, decisions that may have resulted in a very good outcome and positive feedback for us in the simpler decision system—for example, the decision to take it easy and not work too hard—can be translated by the organization into quite another feedback—for example, "You're fired!"

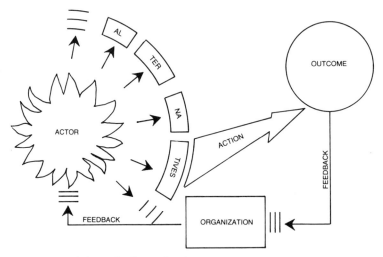

Figure H: Decisions in Organizations

Why submit to collective organization then? The reason, as we have seen in our analysis of collusion in Chapter Two, is that organization enables us to do what is difficult or impossible to do singly. For example, the family organization allows us to give birth to and raise up children. The large corporation enables us to do what is difficult to do even in small groups: design, build, finance, and market computers or aircraft or a television broadcast network. The large commune or governmental unit can accomplish what individuals can only contemplate in their dreams: an interstate highway system, an army or a navy, an Aswan dam, a system of public education, and so on. Humans are social animals. We have always worked together. And if our needs are relatively obvious, such as our need for self defense and security, our need for the control of rampaging flood waters, our need for organized systems for the supply of life's basic necessities, or our need for the reproduction of our own species, our own individual goals are often synonymous with those of our organizations. Under these circumstances, we may expect to be well served by our governments, our enterprises, and our families. (But even then we may be disappointed. History shows us very few instances of lasting harmony between individuals and their organizations.)

Certainly life is not that simple in the developed economies. Our needs are often much less obvious and much less easily agreed upon. Furthermore, many organizations are not dedicated to being totally responsive to the preferences of all the people whom they touch. We would expect a monarchy or a dictatorship or a mafia mob to cater to the wishes of the king or boss first, before anyone else is considered. Corporations also tend to put their managements' preferences ahead of those of their workers, stockholders, and customers. Communes, collectives, and cooperatives also favor some preferences—those associated with their leaders or their ideology—over others.

Even if our organizations did represent our preferences as well as possible, whether through participatory democracy, through some benign and intelligent elite rule, or through a federal system, each organization must operate from an average of all our individual preferences. At its best, this averaging will accurately articulate a central tendency at the cost of individual differences. At its worst, it can be more brutally simplistic, either reflecting our preferences in the distorting mirror of some ruling elite or simply expressing the lowest common denominator of all the individual preferences.

No wonder, then, that these larger organizations often appear to lumber on in their set direction, like a drunk with his liquor, unresponsive to changes in the outcome of their actions. Their feedback loops are numbed to anything but gross averages, the conventions of the ruling establishment, and/or the safely lowest common denominator. In their inability to perceive any signals to the contrary, they cannot judge when enough is enough, and we find ourselves, like so many puppets on a string, the unwilling participants in organized activities that can only be described as pathological.

Examples abound. American commercial television, whose programming is deplored by one and all, comes immediately to mind. It blunders on from season to season in its full blown banality, unable to respond to anything but the most homogenized and common feedback signals. Nationally franchised quick food chains, giant universities, the large international retail and mail order department store chains, federal welfare agencies, communist and socialist bureaucracies, and, of course, all organizations that conscript us into the nine to five lockstep make us suffer the same malady. As consumers we have to accept goods and services intended for everyone in general, which means for no one in particular; as workers we have to conform to conditions intended to suit everyone in general, which also means that they will probably suit no one in particular. Our unique personal preferences remain irrelevant.*

Profits and Priorities.

So far, our marginal analysis has scrupulously measured

---

*The same analysis has noneconomic applications as well. The highly organized U.S. military involvement in Viet Nam may be a classic case. Even though it eventually became apparent to almost everyone individually, including Vietnamese, American soldiers, American citizens at home, politicians, and advisors, that the American effort was reaping very rapidly diminishing returns and incurring rapidly increasing costs, the military involvement continued. In spite of demonstrations, desertions, self immolations, and military defeats in battle, the military-political complex could not seem to respond to the message. Its feedback communications were effectively cut.

costs and returns in terms of preferences or satisfactions, which, in any final analysis, are the only coin of value. Money, which is an averaged common denominator of value intended for everyone in general, cannot possibly denominate value accurately at all times for anyone in particular. Yet money is such a convenient measure and store of value and such a convenient medium of exchange that it is generally used—at least as an intermediate unit of account—especially when economic decisions are taken through organizations. Even in centrally controlled collectivized economies, where aggregated nonmonetary priorities may find a stronger voice in economic analyses and business management, success is still largely measured in terms of monetary criteria. In fact, economists have been accused of knowing "the price of everything, and the value of nothing".

The decision procedure using money is deceptively similar to the procedure that deals directly in satisfactions. The work vs. leisure decision analysis outlined in non-monetary terms in Figure F could become a monetary decision simply by putting dollar signs in front of each of the numerical quantities and retitling the column headings accordingly. Suppose, for example, that we are deciding how to spend sixteen dollars (instead of hours: "time is money", too) on either radio or newspaper advertising for puppies that we have for sale. In the column headings write *dollars* in place of hours, *revenues* in place of returns, *radio advertising* in place of work, and *newspaper advertising* in place of leisure. Every dollar spent on radio advertising is denied newspaper advertising, and vice versa. Again the optimum proportion happens to come where the marginal revenues (marginal returns, in the original) of both alternatives are equal. That is, according to our table, it would produce the largest grand total revenue, $24.90, to spend eight dollars each on radio and newspaper advertising. Our profits—the money we clear out of this deal—are ($24.90 - $16.00) eight dollars and ninety cents. And our limited budget of time and space, now expressed as a fund of money, is allocated to alternative productive uses in a way that maximizes our fund of money.

The revenue gained through newspaper advertising

would be the opportunity cost of radio advertising, or seen just as well the other way around, the revenue gained through radio advertising would be the opportunity cost of newspaper advertising. Opportunity costs are the only real costs of any action. That is, in economic decision behavior, as in so much of life, everything is relative. (Even growing old is a wonderful thing, when you consider the only other available alternative.) And to speak of the cost of something simply in its dollars and cents price, as if that were the definitive evaluation, is to short circuit the analysis almost before it is begun. A thing—an act, a decision—costs not its price but what has to be forgone because of it.

The trouble is that money is ubiquitous. It is so wonderfully convenient to use and so easy to understand that it often subverts our attempts to evaluate our decisions in the more accurate terms of opportunity costs and the most accurate terms of personal preferences and satisfactions. Like the use of cliches in our language, the use of money in evaluation is handy, effortless, and often reasonably effective. But also like the use of cliches, using monetary values as an easy substitute for real evaluations to determine our decisions is a depravity of thought that leads to serious distortions. On an individual level, overvaluing "the mighty dollar" leads to equating price with value, salary with standard of living, and marketable investments with personal wealth. Perhaps the substantive purchasing power of the dollar is not even so much at issue as its symbolic power. As such, it becomes the index of our success, and some of us may actually deprive ourselves for it, getting ulcers for a higher salary or losing our grace and self-esteem for profits.

On this individual level, the distortions are tragic or comic, depending on their scope and our point of view. We can always hope that those who are so afflicted will soon come to their senses. On the organizational level, the affliction may be much more serious. First, if monetary evaluation is a kind of convenient cliche for individuals, it is 'almost a necessity for organizations. It is the common denominator; it is the universal language that reduces the babel of individual preferences to one dimension of value. Second, by definition, organizational decisions touch many people. So, to the degree that this monetary myopia afflicts organizations—and they are especially vulnerable to it—the priorities of many people, even the national priorities may be distorted. And we have the picture of manufacturing plants polluting their own nests in order to keep costs down, of governments cutting expressways through their most beautiful nature preserves in order to save a few miles of construction, and so on. In all these cases, a complete and balanced economic evaluation of all the needs, preferences, and potential satisfactions would have been much more accurate, but the voice of money is exceedingly loud.

A Question of Horizon.

Another form of myopia that afflicts our decision behavior is a misjudged—usually a falsely foreshortened—time horizon. This is the problem that children experience when they cannot understand that the bitter medicine, whose taste (the immediate outcome) is so unpleasant, will have a very beneficial outcome for them in the longer run. This is also the problem that afflicts some criminals when they forget to deduct the eventual probable punishment from the immediate payoff they expect to get out of their intended crime. This is the problem of the shortsighted excessive consumption of our natural resources that might have been better used in some future application. In sum, it is irresponsibility and waste measured over time.

Yet, none of this is supposed to happen. Accurate and rational decision behavior should be able to take all outcomes into account—the distant future outcomes as well as the more immediate ones—in order to weigh all the available alternatives effectively. Standard elementary economic textbooks teach us that, by carefully calculating with interest rate formulas, we may discount the future outcomes of our economic decisions and translate them into present value equivalents, at which point we can easily compare all available alternatives with each other. For example, suppose we are considering putting one thousand dollars worth of our resources into one of two alternative investments. One is expected to pay back 1,100 dollars at the end of a year, for a ten percent profit. The other would yield only 125 dollars at the end of a year, but would continue to yield that much at the end of every year into perpetuity. Using the formula: annual income ÷ interest rate = present value, and applying the same ten percent of interest to this second alternative too, we find that 125 divided by .10 equals 1250, which is to say, our one thousand dollars acts for us as if it were 1250 dollars in this alternative. Clearly, when future outcomes are accounted for and if risks are the same for both alternatives, the second alternative investment is better than the first. Incisive, isn't it?

The trouble is that evaluating the future is seldom so simple. What is the dollar value of the future income flow from well preserved forests or unused petroleum reserves or even from a family's summer cottage (not for rent, but used by the family) at Indian Lake? These values defy translation into the language of dollars and cents, so what numbers do we plug into the formulas? And how far into the future and into whose future should we gaze in our calculations? Being so inarticulate about the future, is it any wonder that we may prefer the language of the present? That is, we know the satisfactions of our large luxury automobiles. We can feel them and we can evaluate them now. Why trade that for the mute values of having petroleum in an uncertain future inhabited by generations of strangers? And so, to paraphrase a saying, we tend to prefer a bird in hand to one and a tenth (at ten percent annual interest rates) birds in the bush, as irrational and mistaken as that may be at times.

The opposite affliction, that is, overvaluing the future, is not unheard of. There are those for whom life is a saving up in preparation for and in anticipation of the future. We hear of the worst cases occasionally in the news: Perhaps an impoverished old recluse is found dead in a ramshackle home, in which he has squirreled away dozens of rusty cans containing a fortune in moldy dollar bills. Being an economist, I would not venture a psychological opinion on his malady, but economically the recluse is no more crazy than those of us who live only for the here and now.

One of the factors limiting our time horizon is the length of our own life span. There is no point to planting an olive orchard when we are 75 years old unless we are doing it for our children. So it might be argued that the average time horizon for economic decisions would equal the average life span left to the people in decision making capacities in the population, or about forty years in the United States . . . and, after that, let the chips fall where they may. But this is certainly an overestimation of the time horizon for the vast majority of our decisions. We may take forty years and more into account when we choose our marriage partner; we may even be as future minded in our choice of career. Thirty year mortgages are not uncommon in the real estate business. However, businesses rarely calculate more than ten years into the future and their overwhelming concern must necessarily be with "making or breaking it" in the next six months. Politicians can hardly see beyond the next election, and a great many consumers count time from payday to payday.

Some economists have argued that corporations, because they have neither the biological mortality of live people nor the political mortality of governments, should be able to have a time horizon that far exceeds any other. Theoretically, then, an outcome a century or more from now should be accounted for in a corporation's decision making, and corporations should be the logical choice as the caretakers of our natural resources, of our environment, of the world in which our future generations will have to live. Experience does not seem to bear this out, however. First of all, corporations are not immortal. They can be bought out and merged with other corporations, and they can become bankrupt. Stockholders and their elected representatives on the boards of directors are also not immortal. But most important, the management people making corporate policy hardly feel immortal at all. Their jobs are on the line. If they cannot produce an immediate or nearly immediate payoff, they will probably not survive a year in which to contemplate the next century.*

The one organization that may be considered to invoke a longer-than-human time horizon at times is the family. As we shall see in the next chapter, what happens to our children and even their children's children *does* make a difference to us, under some circumstances. This not only lengthens the decision horizon but powerfully changes the scenery it contains.

---

*This brings up an important point. There is a tendency for economists to analyze families, firms, and governments as if they were autonomous organisms, somehow miraculously quickened with their own life and thought. Entomologists suggest that a swarm of bees or ants can function more like a real brain than can a single bee or ant. Early sociologists hailed bureaucracy as the instrument which, by sanitizing the behavior of individual humans, would subordinate them to the rational purposes of the organization, making us function in the organization like a bee or an ant or like a cell in the tissues of our bodies, forfeiting all personal preferences and desires in the assumption of our bureaucratic roles.

We can be skeptical. Perhaps when computers become so complex that they achieve a life of their own, like the computer named Hal in the story *2001*, this may be possible. In the meantime, the actions of any organization are nothing more and nothing less than the actions of people working within the framework of the organization. This is not simplistic reductionism, but hard nosed reality.

In the final account, people must necessarily and by definition try to serve their own interests. Should their own interests and those of their organization converge, that is more an indication that the organization serves these people well than that the people serve the organization well. Should there interests not converge, the unhappy disharmony is not caused by the organization or the "system" but by other people within the same organization who are using it for their own contrary purposes.

CHAPTER 4

Staying Rich

The Power of Income.

"This land is your land, this land is my land," goes the song, voicing a generous sentiment that is honored more in the breach than in the observance by all living species, including man. Competition for the economic environment is seldom gentle and never finished. As emphasized in Chapter Two, the proprietary transformation is the primary determinant of "who owns what", and, as such, is the main vehicle through which the ideological posture—the mix of collectivism and free enterprise—of any economy is expressed. But, regardless of the particular ideology an economy may have and regardless of the discrimination, theft, chicanery, and abuse of free goods that may interfere, the proprietary transformation always does somehow take place. To the degree that we use anything, we also claim it. If they are to become attached to the economic process, the economic resources of the environment must be transformed into owned resources somehow.

The question then is, how are these resources claimed? How do we make the strongest competitive bid for a particular resource? And the answer that applies to all economies is:

The more successfully we have used the opportunities of the economic environment in the past, the stronger will be our present claims on that environment now. The past performance of an individual, corporation, family, cooperative, production ministry, nation, or global economic unit determines its present share. Of course, this is a familiar story and applies universally to all life processes. The more successfully anything can survive and thrive, the better is its chance of continued survival and growth. This holds good, whether the organism is simple or complex, plant or animal, person or society.

Our analysis, as always, proceeds with people in mind. The key to the proprietary claim, in human-economic terms, is to understand the dynamic nature of income. To be sure, the end purpose of all economic activity is the satisfactions that will result from income. But these satisfactions are not the only result of the economic process. Indeed, they could not be, unless they were in the nature of a "last reward", after which all further activity ceased. Instead, income is also used as the source of the energy, substance, and information needed for all the transformations in the economic sequence. These quantities are not so much the end as they are the beginning of the economic process.

To provide this beginning, these quantities have to be produced from those forms of income that enhance our ability and performance. They should give us mental alertness, physical health, energy, stamina, accumulations of technology and knowledge, accumulations of tangible and intangible property, and cultural values amenable to economic production. Such positive forms of income are not a foregone conclusion; we often take our pleasures in less wholesome ways. Drugs, alcohol, superstitions, other wordly mysticisms, and a whole catalogue of devious gratifications and foolishnesses have exercised their counterproductive influences on our individual and collective economic processes throughout history. Although many of these enjoy periods when they are freely tolerated or even heralded as "the new truth", they extract their toll. For some of us, our very survival may be threatened by the resulting misjudgment, exhaustion, and impoverishment.

Accentuating the problem is the fact that, just like nature, the economic process abhors a vacuum. We cannot long afford the luxury of incompetence. Our environment is ultimately limited, and the resources we are able to recognize therein at any one time and at any one state of technology are even more exactly limited. So, should an individual—you or I, a corporation, or other agency—not be able to take advantage of an opportunity immediately, should we not be able to afford the price, expend the energy, or commit the resources necessary to claim a desired part of the environment, it will not wait for us. Somebody else or some other agency will always claim it. This is necessarily so because the price of these elements of the environment, the amount of energy and material resources that has to be spent to claim them, is relative. It is established by the competing claims of all the economic actors for these elements, as if by auction. Thus, in an active, striving economy, no potential resource is ignored, no possible opportunity is unexamined, and no vacuum can remain unfilled for long. And, barring other interventions (a considerable qualification, since interventions are not at all unlikely), the environment is claimed by those who can exert the strongest claim by dint of their successful past economic performance.

This should come as no surprise. Everyone knows that a high income is the architect of wealth and that wealth is itself a source of high income. Some people inherit wealth or marry money or strike it rich by an accidental find of some kind, but, as a universal economic principle, wealth originates from produced income, that is to say, it is earned. Before going any further, we must emphasize that money income, the conventional measure of economic performance, is only a partial and intermediate yardstick. It is intermediate because we must first exchange it for goods and services which we must ultimately transform into our satisfactions via the consumption transformation. And it is partial because, even in advanced industrialized and commercialized economies, only a fractional part of our total satisfactions can be bought by spending money on goods and services. Most realistically, then, income is defined as the inflow of satisfactions that we derive from all the goods and services produced by the economic activity at our command. The store of these goods and services, our accumulations of owned resources, is our wealth. Income is the flow; wealth is the fund.

The distinction between flow and fund, however, is not always clear and not always functional. Generally we think of income as either being "consumed"—taken in the form of satisfactions—or "saved"—accumulated in the form of owned resources. But many of the satisfactions from consumed income also behave like a store of wealth. For example, even the most intangible and fleeting satisfaction, such as the pleasure of hearing a symphony (or whatever kind of music we prefer) concert, endows us with a mental feeling of enrichment, a feeling of "having been to a concert" that probably lasts us longer than the musical performance itself. "The song has ended, but the melody lingers on," and this having-been-to-a-concert feeling may even be considered a source of strength, a source of psychic sustenance that will enable us to carry out our other functions in the economic sequence more effectively, perhaps forever, but at least until we get the feeling that we need to go to a concert again. Furthermore, the joy of owning, that is, the promise of potential satisfactions to be derived from accumulations of various kinds of property is, in itself, a satisfaction. Many people find that owning a house is somehow more satisfying to them than renting it, even though owning may be less convenient or more expensive.

All these satisfactions contribute to or are synonymous with our very substance as economic actors. They represent that body of value which, when we apply it in the form of transformation energies, helps to determine how well we are able to produce, consume, and carry on the economic sequence. And, most important to the analysis here, they enable us to make proprietary claims. The more such satisfactions have contributed to our well-being, our strength, and our vitality, the more powerful will be our claims.

Learning, Dying, and the Law Again.

So, do "the rich get richer" ("and the poor get children"), as another song goes? If income creates wealth and wealth creates income, will one super-rich economic actor eventually end up owning all the limited economic environment? So far, it has not happened, at least not on a global scale. But the concentration of monopolies and the fear of the absolute power that "corrupts absolutely" are old and familiar threats. Indeed, these threats provide the rationale for a great deal of ideologically motivated policy. For example, both the egalitarianism of collectivist economies and the antitrust legislation in free enterprise economies are addressed to this concern. But before we deal with these policies, let us examine the nonideological forces inherent in all economic processes that mute the tendency towards concentration. Underlying these forces again is the familiar law of eventually diminishing marginal returns.

Real wealth can be accumulated only in actual specific forms, such as particular stocks and bonds; ownership of certain houses and land acreages; knowledge about a particular delimited art, science, or business; collections of unique, valuable objects; an establishment of a particular pattern of business practices and connections; a large accumulation of money savings held in specific savings accounts; and so on. Even the broadest investment portfolio or the most extensive collection of art objects or global real estate holdings is still just that: shares in this and that company, bonds of this local government and that railroad, particular art objects, or land and buildings located somewhere. We may be careful enough not to put all our eggs in one basket, but we do have to put the eggs in some baskets somewhere. That is, real accumulations, real investments are real commitments, and that is good enough for the long arm of the law of eventually diminishing marginal returns.

Accumulations of wealth do not have their productivity rate engraved in stone. Like all productive activities, they are subject to the risk that the economic environment will no longer be as productive or as salable as it once was. Indeed, the productive accumulation—the investment—itself may be the cause of the environmental change. Of course, good investment managers are aware of this and bend every effort to keep large accumulations of wealth as fungible as possible. That is, they try to maintain their capability to move the wealth from one form to another and to spread it around in a variety of ways whenever it seems advantageous to do so. This mobility of wealth is called *liquidity,* and the most liquid, most mobile form of wealth is money. But, desirable as liquidity is, it is usually achieved at the expense of economic leverage. The more liquid and diffuse our holdings are, the less we can use them as an active tool for our economic ends; the less productive they are. It may be safer; but the less ventured, the less gained. So the temptation is strong to concentrate on one or a very few baskets, taking the too-many-eggs risk into the bargain.

History affords many examples: not long ago investments in the fur trade, cotton agriculture, railroading, oil drilling, steelmaking, photographic film manufacture, and automobiles—to name just a few—created extraordinary fortunes for families and stockholders. Today their income productivity has waned or is, at least, no longer very remarkably superior. Had these family accumulations of wealth been rigidly locked onto the very industries by which they were created, they too would have declined. The historical evidence seems to indicate that most of them were sufficiently mobile to escape this fate. But, as we have seen, this mobility (liquidity) can take its toll in lost vigor and productivity. In other times, when the income that produced wealth was more fixedly based on such resources as soil fertility or populations of fish and game, any deterioration of this base brought about by events, such as changes in climate, changes in ocean currents, or overuse, would cause a decline of both income and wealth and perhaps would even lead to the extinction of the people themselves, whether they were primitive clans or tribes or even rather grand city states and nations. Where are the once thriving people of Babylon or of any other long lost ancient economy today? Indeed, where is the rich economy that once was an ample tax base for New York City?

So the law of eventually diminishing marginal returns does work against the limitless concentration of economic wealth and power. But many of us are not completely reassured. Perhaps we can still feel the hot breath of somebody else's concentrated wealth and power down our necks. When we think of our powerful governments, corporations, unions, and banks, of the monolithic bureaucracies in universities, governmental agencies, schools and hospitals, and of the established wealth of our rich families, we wonder whether the key word in the law is *eventually*, indeed, *very* eventually.

Maybe it will reassure us to know that there are other limits to the accumulation of wealth. One of the most absolute is death. Of course, the death of the owner does not change the physical nature of real and tangible accumulations of wealth. (Remember that the proprietary transformation is always depicted as an arrow drawn with a dashed line to emphasize this point.) The accumulations may be bequeathed to the next owners; inheritance laws provide for the offspring to receive the parents' wealth. But this transfer of accumulations from one generation to the next at the time of death is also a time of great vulnerability for wealth. Not only may the wealth be dissipated among too many heirs, but the event of death provides a unique opportunity for the society to intervene with taxes and other assessments to express its ideological preferences about the concentration of economic wealth and power. Generally we would expect collectivist economies, with their strong egalitarian preferences, to prevent this transfer to the next generation most rigorously, so that as little unearned wealth as possible would exist. They should have the steepest inheritance tax rates. Yet virtually all modern economies, collectivist or not, intervene in the inheritance process in some way with egalitarian intent.

But death goes further than this. First, many forms of wealth are not efficiently transferred from person to person or from generation to generation under any ideological circumstance. For example, certain acquired social, economic, and psychological qualities help produce a great fortune or a position of great power, but they do not transfer very well to the next generation of inheritors. We can try to pass on our money, stocks, bonds, real estate, and even our social position to our children; it is much harder to try to pass on (or to try *not* to pass on) our wit, talent, charm, and intelligence. And second, wealth may sow the seeds of its own destruction. The easy life created by an established fortune and power may tend to undermine those very qualities which created the wealth originally. The Biblical story of the prodigal son has a happier ending than it often has in our own world.

However, although death may be an egalitarian boon, it is an efficiency bust. Probably nothing hinders the progress of an underdeveloped economy more painfully than a high mortality rate, which can regularly kill off half the population before it reaches a productive age. The food, clothing, shelter, education, care, love, and hope that were embodied in these victims are a horrendous cost and an anguishing loss. Almost as tragic is the way in which death destroys the accumulations of intangible wealth—skills and knowledge, cultural accomplishments, and patterns of social and economic relationships—in all economies. Societies make valiant attempts to salvage these intangible accumulations by various systems of education. The more sophisticated of these attempts can themselves consume almost half a lifetime, leaving little time to build new knowledge on top of old. Information storage and retrieval systems have been employed throughout human history, from clay tablets to electronic data processing machines, in an effort to snatch accumulations of knowledge away from the grip of mortality. But no such system has had more than imperfect success.

In the end, we always have to create much knowledge anew anyway. Not only has much of it died a natural death, but also, in a changing, evolving world, much has to be created for the first time. This rediscovery of old knowledge and the searching for new knowledge are very important aspects of all economic activity. A substantial part of all our efforts, energies, and material resources spent on making the economy go is spent on the learning process. For example, we cannot truly maximize the outcome of a decision by a blind optimization of proportions from a given catalogue of available alternatives. Instead, we must always be on the look out for new and better available alternatives. Only this will assure us that the optimal proportions achieved by our decisions will also achieve the maximum possible returns. A very important part of the entire economic endeavor, then, is the seeking out of new sources of returns, the evaluating of new opportunities, and the discovering of new vacuums to be filled. And another name for this is learning.

That economic learning often appears to be the businesslike behavior of producers and consumers in the everyday world, rather than the scholarly behavior of students in a classroom or library, does not deny the fact that the two kinds of behavior are essentially the same. Their purpose is also the same. Whether the learning develops useful skills or leads to better homemaking, better business management, a taste for better music and cuisine, the discovery of extraterrestrial resources, or a deepening of philosophical wisdom, the process is always to discover and evaluate new ideas and realities and to rediscover old ones. Its purpose is always and ultimately to increase our efficiency, to raise our level of returns, which is to say, to get more out of life.

And so learning is also another barrier to the monopolization of all wealth and power by one actor. It works like the David and Goliath story: David's well placed use of a different alternative (the stone sling) thoroughly undid a large and powerful accumulation (Goliath). David's trick, of course, was to recognize the usefulness of his alternative and to know how to implement it. Perhaps, what is most important about all this is not so much the fact but the *promise* to all the Davids of the world. The promise that they may be able to move in on some wealthy and powerful Goliath is sufficient to keep them searching for better alternatives. We have already seen that another name for this activity is learning. Still another name for it is progress, and progress is the undoing of established accumulations of rigidly immobile wealth and power.

Economic Growth.

Progress is also economic growth. Only three simple ingredients are necessary for economic growth: one, people eager to learn and achieve and—to continue the preceding metaphor—a lot of Davids eager for progress; two, the endowment of these people with a large enough surplus of vital energies and owned resources beyond what they need for simple subsistence so that they are able to take advantage of opportunities when they come knocking and to go in search of them when they do not; and three, the existence of such opportunities. Unfortunately, these three preconditions are so often inadequately met that economic growth and development counts as one of the main unsolved problems of humanity today. Let us examine them one at a time.

To be sure, there seems to be no shortage of the first precondition, the existence of eager people. Almost by definition, to be alive is to be eager, to want to survive, to want to grow. But more specifically, very nearly the entire world today is aware of the advantages offered by the industrialization and commercialization of manufacture and agriculture, the modernization of technology, and the adoption of twentieth-century culture. Almost all of us know that we cannot turn the clock back; only a very few around the world would even want to.

Which is not to say that this "revolution of rising expectations" is universally received as an unmixed blessing. There are some important pockets of resistance to it. One is found in the vested interests of the tradition-bound older generations and the remaining feudal and tribal power structures. To be fair, this is probably not so much a resistance to new economic opportunity as it is a fear of the unknown. People living on small margins of safety cannot afford experiments, and so they are anxious about the real or imagined threats to their own vested interests, their own small proprietary claims and slight accumulations of owned resources. Another resistance is found in the people whose corporations or government agencies have found a comfortable niche in the status quo, and who prefer no change, even if the change is a general improvement. These Goliaths are familiar in every economic landscape, and we have already seen how they may be dealt with.

Lastly, a resistance to economic growth is often voiced by those who fear it means a mindless intensification of industrialism, commercialism, and urban congestion. A blind, headlong rush to expand these patterns of economic production, in fact, may cause more destruction of real and potential satisfactions than it creates. Pollution of the air and water and environmental damage have both become major social and political issues in virtually all economies, undeveloped as well as developed. Less sober opinions have attributed this mismanagement of the economic process to diabolical capitalist profiteering, to a communist fixation on the material, to some failing in the Judeo-Christian morality, or even to a sinister curse of science and technology. Chapter Two presented my analysis of this problem, namely, that the havoc wreaked on our environment is caused mainly by a forfeiture of the proprietary transformation that allows the air, the water, and the scenery to be used and abused free of charge and free of restraint. When real growth is properly managed, it can only be a positive gain to be eagerly sought. Human nature is our guarantee of that.

The second precondition is not nearly as well guaranteed as the first one. There is no assurance that all people everywhere will be endowed with enough surplus energies and owned resources to take advantage of growth opportunities. Many existing economies produce a very tenuous margin of satisfactions beyond those needed to keep their people alive and the economic sequence in minimal operation. Learning and education are a rare luxury; accumulating any kind of productive investment, such as machinery, drainage, irrigation, or hospitals, seems impossible in the face of elemental biological and physical needs that must be met first. Under these circumstances, any deviation from the tried and true patterns of traditional economic sequence carries a heavy threat of disaster, because any trial that results in error, any experiment that fails may quickly destroy the very economic basis on which the people's survival depends. Rigid socioeconomic conservatism and severe reluctance to learn and to grasp new opportunities are perfectly rational responses to this condition, and are the most effective damper on any expression of eagerness for economic growth.

Yet this condition sets the stage for the one most important chance for outside help. Indeed, foreign aid for economic growth can do no better than to provide the extra cushion of satisfactions that will allow accumulation, education, and experimentation to begin. The various programs of direct economic aid to underdeveloped countries, such as food and medical relief, the building and staffing of schools and hospitals, gifts of farm machinery and industrial plants, the construction of dams for hydroelectric and irrigation facilities, the establishment of agricultural experiment stations, technical training programs, or the building of roads, supply exactly those forms of energy and material resources from outside the underdeveloped economy that the underdeveloped country is unable to produce from within. These aids are the cushion of safety. They constitute the surplus on which growth may be based, the luxury of education may be afforded, and experimentation may be risked.

Although international aid may come in many additional guises and for many different motivations, the mechanism by which it exerts its economic effect is always the same: it supplies the extra margin of resources that provides the basis for growth. We will have to admit that even military assistance relieves an underdeveloped economy of all or part of the burden of providing for these things itself and enables it then to take advantage of other opportunities, including those for economic growth and development. Foreign financial assistance, such as release from foreign debts and extension of favorable credit terms for the purchase of foreign goods, will have the same effect. It helps to relieve the underdeveloped economy of the burden of generating its own international financial strength, usually done by selling its products abroad, and enables it to use these resources instead for its efforts at economic development at home.

These kinds of indirect economic aid, especially the financial aid, are sometimes preferred to direct economic assistance, because they seem to give the underdeveloped economy itself a greater autonomy in designing its own economic development and finding its own opportunities. Furthermore, these aids are often politically more convenient for both the giving country and the receiving one.

The third precondition for economic growth and development, the existence of opportunities, is neither guaranteed, like the first, nor available, if needed, through outside help like the second. When basic economic opportunities, such as those provided by fertile agricultural land, an adequate climate, or access to the sea or to mineral deposits, are absent, there is very little that can be done about it. Of course, the environment that supports economic activity would include many other kinds of resources, including cultural achievements and human strengths, that might be substituted for the missing ones. But these intangible resources, since they themselves embody mostly the education, the technology, and the industrial and commercial sophistication that can be created only out of an economic surplus, are best developed in context with an adequate supply of the basic physical resources.

Even little Switzerland, so often used as Exhibit A for making something out of nothing, has beautiful scenery for tourism, a rather productive agriculture, and such a long history of economic integration with its immediately adjacent neighbors that its economy developed simultaneously with theirs. Or Israel, that made the desert "blossom as the rose", in fact did so through a massive importation of just those cultural and human resources that could not have been created by the indigenous economy alone. While such discoveries as oil in North Africa and Alaska and iron ore in the Congo feed the myth of untold riches in the jungles, deserts, and frozen wastes of the world, they are exceptions to the rule. Most of these areas will support very little economic activity and only a very sparse population because they are resource-poor and are likely to remain so in the foreseeable future.

Discoveries of a single rich resource in a previously poor area, such as oil in the Middle East, are not a foolproof key to economic development anyway, contrary to the hopes and dreams aroused by such discoveries. Economic development proceeds best as an integrated organic whole, with all the main sectors of the economy—agriculture, industry, commerce, finance, research and development, and so on—participating together. A single rich resource can do little to unlock the grip of backwardness in the other sectors of the economy, unless the physical potential for their development already exists. For example, medieval Spain was able to parlay its New World discoveries of gold into vast riches for itself, by buying naval stores, military goods and services, and consumer goods from the surrounding countries. But, when the gold flow ebbed and finally shut off, Spain was left with little more than memories of its grandeur, while the surrounding countries were left with thriving industries *and* the gold. Only the most extraordinarily sophisticated guidance of economic growth and a lot of good luck can prevent a similar fate from eventually befalling today's underdeveloped oil exporting nations.

Nevertheless, a country's endowment of resources need not be its final and irrevocable sentence in the court of economic fates. While the occurence of most physical resources is immovably fixed in geologic neartime, the economic definition of what is and what is not a resource is much more dynamic. New technology may some day enable us to make rocket fuel out of sea shells and sheet metal out of lawn clippings, turning the beach and the front lawn into valuable resource sites. So, even though the geographic dimensions and elemental composition of our global and solar environment are rigidly delimited, the opportunities for economic growth need not be, especially if this growth is not necessarily predicated on quantitative increases in the gross production of material goods, but is defined as an increase in real human well-being.

And so the competitive search for new vacuums to fill

need never diminish. Subject to the conditions of mortality, the restraints of the law of eventually diminishing returns, and this eager striving to learn of new economic opportunities, income will continue to create wealth. The economic process will continue to be consonant with the life process, in the sense that those whose economic performances are the most effective will derive the most satisfactions from it. And to the extent that there are increases in the number and degree of such effective economic performers, the whole economy itself will grow and become more effective. At least, this is the basic premise.

CHAPTER 5

From Person
to Person

The Human Interface.

Production and consumption, spurred by our drive for survival and growth and curbed by the law of eventually diminishing marginal returns, are the only real transformation of materials and energies in the economic sequence. Only they create the new goods and services from which satisfactions must ultimately be obtained.

By contrast, the proprietary transformation and the transfer-or-exchange transformation involve no new creation of goods and services, but only a change in ownership. Yet, they also contribute to the economy's ability to create satisfactions for us. In the case of the proprietary transformation, this is accomplished by introducing the needed parts of the environment into the economic sequence; in the case of the transfer-or-exchange transformation, it is done by redistributing the ownership of produced goods and services in order that we may get the most satisfactions out of them. And, like all the transformations in the economic process, these must abide by the need to economize: that is, they need to seek the best rate of returns among all available alternatives.

The transfer-or-exchange transformation, more than any other, deals directly with interpersonal relations. It is the transformation of interfaces between people. The importance of other people to the individual in the economic process is not ignored by the remaining transformations. In those transformations, other people have usually been considered as part of the economic environment, as factors, as suppliers of some important and useful commodity or as competitors for the environment or for a share of the economy's output. But in the transfer-or-exchange transformation, other people are more often the *subjects* of the transformation, in some cases they are even the mutually motivated cooperators who share in the gains to be derived from the transformation.

The human interface seems to exist on two distinct content levels. One is the communicative level, in which information flows between the participants. While relatively minor efforts are needed to express and retain this information in some medium of communication and storage, (nicely described by cyberneticians as "Kleinstrommechanik", microwatt mechanics), the information content of the communication is essentially free of cost. When one person gives information to another, he still retains the original information; it is not lost to him. Thus, a teacher does not become more ignorant as he shares his knowledge with his students; and, once a copy of this book is printed and distributed, the publisher and I will bear no extra costs should it be read by ten or even fifty people. A teacher's salary or the price of this book, then, are not so much payments for the ideas communicated as they are reimbursement of the teacher's opportunity cost (see page 37) and payment for the production costs of the book, the paper, and so on.

Therefore, information need not be economized; it can be freely squandered. And interpersonal relations that take place purely on the communicative level are not subject to economic analysis, except as regards the returns and costs of the media of communication employed. It is one of the greatest strengths of our species *homo sapiens* that its main instrument for survival and growth is the *sapiens* aspect of it, the knowledge aspect, because, while creating and transmitting new information is costly, the use and reuse of existing information and knowledge is free and unlimited, a wellspring of sustenance that never runs dry.

The other level of interpersonal relationship is the flow of materials and energies and of goods and services between people. Here what one of us gains the other must give up, because the substance of the exchange is tangible.

Grants.

There are three reasons why we will knowingly and purposely transfer some of our accumulation of owned resources and goods and services to someone else. One such reason is love or, at least, some positive sensation of goodwill and community. In a transaction motivated by such benevolence, we will grant some of our accumulated resources, goods, and/or services to the object of our sentiment. Since this transfer is voluntary, we must assume that it is the best choice among our various alternatives and that we act the way we do simply because we want to. This, in turn, implies that we must somehow expect to receive enough compensation for our act to place us on a higher satisfaction level after the transaction has been successfully completed.

Economic analysis is not the best technique to apply to the psychological and romantic aspects of love, but it is probably safe to say that the compensation the giver gets in return for giving is the satisfaction of having expressed himself somehow. Parents grant their children food, clothing, shelter, and "TLC" because they want to, because it is "the right thing to do", perhaps because it is instinctive, and only incidentally because it may be illegal not to. Governments initiate programs that transfer money, goods, and services to their citizens because it is good politics. Businesses sometimes give their clients gifts because it is good customer relations. More cynical analysts might declare these grants to be purchases of the recipients' return affections, bribes, or even disguised forms of proprietary claims. Whatever the case may be, we know that a grant, by definition, must be voluntary; that the giver cannot be assumed to lose net satisfactions through the transaction, except by mistake; and that the recipient must receive something of value.

Furthermore, conventional economic analysis would lead us to expect that the degree of gift giving—the size of the grant—will be so adjusted that the returns from giving the last incremental increase in the amount of the gift will just equal the returns forfeited by not using this marginal amount of the gift for other purposes. For example, I would give you a gift of a certain value, because doing so gives me satisfaction. Giving you less would give me perceptibly less satisfaction than I save on the cost of the gift. Giving you more would cost me more than the extra satisfaction I would get from it. So the amount I choose to give you maximizes the net return of satisfactions I derive from making the grant. With a little paraphrasing and redefinition, we could set up a table for gift giving decisions like the work-leisure decision table in Figure F.

At first glance, the receiver too would seem to move up to a higher level of satisfaction. Under normal circumstances, the receipt of gratuitous goods and services should be a positive gain for the receiver. However, the gift may also carry an unwelcome obligation with it, an obligation to repay the gift with goodwill or affection or some other recompense that will detract from the gift's potential for satisfaction. The detraction may even be bad enough so that the recipient would rather refuse the gift or, if he had to, would accept it in the unhappy knowledge that he has been victimized by a particularly hypocritical form of theft.

The problem with the grant transaction is that the receiver is essentially an involuntary participant. He or she may have hinted broadly about it, even indicated what was wanted and how much, but in the end the recipient's role is, by definition, passive. There is no mechanism in the transaction to guarantee that the recipient will receive exactly what he wants or the quantity he wants. Nor is there a mechanism in this form of transaction that will direct the gift giver to the particular gift receiver who either wants or needs it most.

This gratuitous and one-sided aspect of a relationship motivated by love, good will, and a sense of community is its basic source of inefficiency. It does not allow all parties to economize, to maximize the returns received from their expenditures of material and energy, to optimize the proportions of owned resources and claims on the environment. Yet the grant transaction is a very important, perhaps the most important, format according to which we will knowingly and purposely transfer some of our accumulation of owned resources, goods, and services to another. For example, practically the entire transfer of goods and services from parents to their children is of this type. Voluntary giving to charities, lending a helping hand to a neighbor, giving that little extra ounce of effort on the job, "performing beyond the call of duty" in the military services, working gratis for the Boy Scouts, the local PTA, environmental groups, political parties, and so on, are all grants. And the benevolent and welfare minded transfers of money, goods, and services between governments or philanthropic institutions and their citizens are also grants. We can safely say that, where an absence of love, goodwill, and sense of community make grants completely impossible, an economy simply could not function.

In spite of its basic economic inefficiency, this kind of transaction seems to work quite well, especially when it is routinized or incorporated into the predictable behavior patterns of established social custom, as it usually is in families, communities, and governmental units. Perhaps, like an old shoe, something that is used every day begins to fit quite comfortably. And as for the grants that are not daily routine, such as those motivated by truly romantic love, economic efficiency is hardly a valid criterion anyway. In the end, grants are probably here to stay. Arguing about their efficiency boils down to a consideration of the applicability of alternative means of transferring goods and services from one person to another, but most parents will continue to provide their little children with room and board free of charge, as a gift.

Threats

Another transaction in which we may knowingly and purposely transfer some of our accumulation of owned resources, goods, and services to another is quite the opposite of love, namely threat. The content of this transaction is initiated not by the issuer but by the receiver. That is, it begins with a promise (a threat) from someone forcibly to transfer some drastically negative forms of energy and material to us, his victim, unless we issue to him the positive goods and services in a prescribed manner. Thus, a burglar will threaten to impose knife or bullet wounds on us unless we turn the combination lock, open the safe, and hand over all the money.

Like the grant transaction, threat behavior may sometimes have an important heroic content, a feature that makes economic analysis of it incomplete. But to the degree that threat behavior is rational, the only justification for the transaction is that it is the best choice among the various alternatives available. Someone wants to make the threat because he expects to receive enough compensation for his act to place him on a higher level of satisfaction after the transaction has been successfully completed. Once again it would seem to be a decision in which various alternatives are compared and the potential returns are weighed against the opportunity costs. And, perhaps, the table in Figure F could once again be relabled to supply an hypothetical arithmetic. But conventional marginal analysis does not help us understand the size or amount of the threat transaction, except in a grossly approximate way. The expected marginal returns, which usually figure so prominently in this kind of analysis, defy accurate enumeration in threat transactions. The outcomes, particularly of criminal threat, are very difficult to predict. "All Hell may break loose!", and there is little that can be said here about the amounts that optimize the transaction, beyond admitting that there are smaller threats and larger threats, just as there are misdemeanors and felonies and small-time hoodlums and big-time racketeers.

A threat transaction need not be criminal. Parents use threats, even threats of mild violence, to coerce their children—to eat their vegetables, to bathe properly, to bring the car back before two in the morning, or whatever the family's seasons bring—thereby producing a higher level of

satisfaction for themselves and coincidentally an often il-
lusionary extra satisfaction that they are doing it "for the
children's own good". Teachers threaten their pupils with a
variety of punishments toward the same end; bosses threaten
employees, not always benevolently; governments collect
taxes and conscript soldiers under threat of imprisonment;
and slavery, which is based primarily on threat, has been
legal throughout most of human history.

What all threat transactions have in common is that they
are guaranteed to be economically inefficient. Unless we
admit the special case of masochistic perversity, a threat is
always a deduction from the victim's satisfaction level. Of
course, we may safely agree that the threatener expects to
gain significantly in terms of real and potential satisfactions.
That is why he initiates the transaction. But we may also
safely say that the victim always loses, even though we can
predict nothing about his economic status and preferences,
since his presence in the transaction is always unwilling. In
the unlikely event that accurate interpersonal comparisons of
value were possible, there would still be no mechanism in
the threat transaction that could assure us that the victim's
loss will be less than the threatener's gain. Thus, the net
satisfaction productivity of the transaction for all participants
may be quite negative, even in the best of circumstances.

Furthermore, if the victim does not give in, and the
threat is carried out, then the victim certainly loses a great
deal, and the threatener still has no guarantee of gain. In this
case, the threat transaction can become very sloppy and
totally counterproductive. The burglar, in the above example, will have expended his energies, his bullets, and his
(perhaps) formerly noncriminal status, and we, the victims,
will have suffered possibly fatal wounds. But we may have
successfully defended the locked safe to the end, and with no
transfer of money, all parties, including the burglar, will be at
a lower level of satisfaction than before the transaction was
initiated. Continuing this gruesome anecdote further, and
disregarding questions about the value of criminal justice,
this threat transaction may become disastrously counter-
productive if the criminal is apprehended and punished. If,

in the end, we are murdered, the criminal is duly hung by the neck until dead, and the money is forgotten in the unopenable safe, we must admit the transaction turned out to be a real flop.

Threat transactions need not result in such a dismal outcome. As good economists, we know that everything is relative. A threat transaction may be the best alternative available. For example, sociobiologists—the students of animal social behavior—tell us that threat is often used by chimpanzees, as well as other species, to prevent the actual fighting and killing for food, territory, and mates that takes place among less sophisticated animals. In this sense, a threat is preferable to the real thing, just as being threatened by a burglar with a gun is better than being shot by him outright. But let us not be overgrateful for small favors. In general, threats remain inefficient or even negative satisfaction producers. These transactions are not to be recommended as a form of economic interpersonal relationship. Where they are used extensively as the basic orientation of social relations, the society suffers a malignancy. Anthropologists have described the havoc and disintegration experienced by threat oriented tribes, such as the Yanomamo Indians of South American and the Dobu islanders of Melanesia. The sad columns of refugees from our modern dictatorial regimes indicate the satisfaction productivity of these societies by the direction in which the refugees point their feet. Indeed, common as they are, threat transactions do seem to be used mostly as a last resort, when it is perceived that all other forms of transaction will not suffice.

Exchanges

The third reason for a transfer transformation is exchange. We will knowingly and purposely transfer some of our wealth—some of our accumulation of owned resources, goods, and services—to somebody else or some other group in order to exchange this wealth for real and potential satisfactions that this other party can provide to us. In other words, we give in order to get. In its simplest form, an exchange transaction merely assumes that somebody wants some resource, good, or service belonging to somebody else badly enough to offer something of his own in exchange for it, and that the somebody else is agreeable to the deal. The voluntary participation of both parties is guaranteed by the definition of a successful exchange as a transaction in which both participants get what they want.

Generations of economics students, reciting the litany of "demand and supply", have the impression that exchange is *all* that economics is about. As we have seen, this definition does not even come close to the mark. But because the exchange transaction is voluntary all around and because the participants are, therefore, likely to have rational reasons for their participation, the exchange transaction is particularly amenable to thorough economic analysis. And, in fact, it occupies a substantial proportion of all proper economic analysis, from elementary through the most advanced.

Once again the law of eventually diminishing marginal returns is the main engine of our analysis. This law, let us remember, decrees that the potential returns to be derived from the use of incremental amounts of any one kind of accumulation will diminish as the quantity of it grows in proportion to the whole stock of accumulations owned. Therefore, a mix of accumulations is ultimately preferable to concentration on only one kind. So, should we find ourselves with an overabundance of one kind of accumulation, and, necessarily, an inadequacy of some other kind, it behooves us to try to correct the malproportion. One way we may do this is to adjust our own economic production and consumption activities in such a way that we ourselves can make up the inadequacy and consume the overabundance. In doing so, we may also be gaining some advantages from self-sufficiency, which may be particularly appealing under some circumstances to nations or other group actors who believe they must defend their autonomy and sovereignty in this way. But this tactic ignores an important part of the economic environment, namely, the other people and other groups of people in it. In fact, it may be much more direct and efficient for us to correct the malproportions in our accumulations by participating in exchange transactions with these other economic actors.

An everyday example of this malproportion is the imbalance between accumulated money and accumulated consumer goods and services that results from working for money wages. Again our analysis is the same as that enumerated by the table in Figure F. On payday, we are likely to have more money and fewer consumer goods and services than is optimal, and we will correct this disproportion by spending our money during the following week or month till our next payday. Perhaps this is such a familiar occurrence that it will seem strange to think of a paycheck as a cause of malproportions, but the paycheck itself has little inherent value for us. Only the assurance that it can be exchanged for goods and services makes it worth the effort to earn it. Certainly none of us would show up again for work on Monday if our paychecks had been found to be worthless in the shopping center on the Saturday before.

More specifically, we will begin to spend our money because the returns of satisfaction we expect to get from having money are less than the returns of satisfactions we expect to get from having and using consumer goods and services. And we will continue to spend from our accumulation of money until the marginal returns the money itself provides us are equal to or greater than the marginal returns gained from the consumer good or service we received in exchange for it. (Keeping back some unspent money creates some returns for us, because it provides safety and convenience in case of an emergency or an unexpected opportunity.) At this point, no further adjustment of proportions between money and consumer goods and services is desirable. In other words, the proportions have been optimized.

Of course, our ability to exchange our wages for consumer goods and services is premised on the existence of another economic actor who is willing and able to "buy" our wages from us in exchange for the goods and services. That is, somebody or some organization must exist that has a mix of accumulations that is oppositely malproportioned from our own payday mix, somebody who has too many consumer goods and services relative to money. This other actor's disproportion of accumulations need not be equal, but it must be opposite. Nor do the participants need to have the same urgency or capacity for any particular exchange; they need only to be capable of finding some range within which an exchange is mutually beneficial.

And who is this conveniently opposite somebody else? Obviously, it is our retailers of consumer goods and services, the supermarkets, department stores, mortgage banks, hospitals, schools, and entertainment centers with whom we do business. They will continue to exchange their consumer goods and services for our money according to the same decision rationale that we use, that is, until the returns forfeited by giving up a consumer good or service are no longer less than the returns gained by having more money. And so, in the same way as we do it when we are spending our money, these opposite participants will optimize the proportions of their mix of accumulations. This procedural similarity makes a theoretical distinction between buyer and seller not only unnecessary but also impossible.

However, one real difference between retailers selling consumer goods and services and consumers spending their wages to buy them is that the retailers are not as close to translating all of their decisions into the language of final satisfactions as consumers are. The decisions of the retailers in these exchanges are likely to deal more exclusively in monetary terms. Their decision arithmetic is probably in dollars and cents. When a profit motivated retail manager is adjusting his proportions to the point where the marginal returns from sales equal the marginal returns of inventory held, he is seeking to maximize monetary profits. The marginal returns from sales will consist of the marginal dollar revenues; the marginal returns of maintaining some unsold stock of consumer goods and services (inventory), if, indeed, there are any such returns, might best be considered the potential marginal dollar revenues from selling more advantageously in some other exchange transaction. However, as we saw in Chapter Three, nonmonetary considerations are also important, even to the hardest-bitten profit maximizer, and perhaps more so to the manager in a collectivist economy. Ultimately the results of all decisions are expressed in terms of satisfactions, satisfaction at earning money or earning the most money or increasing the money earnings, satisfactions at meeting or exceeding the revenue quota assigned by the central administrative office, or even the satisfactions from spending the money received. Whatever the case, satisfactions are the final unit of account, even for the persons on the opposite side of the exchange transaction from us.

So by working together in an exchange transaction, everybody can help each other optimize proportions and maximize returns, even if our decision calculus is expressed in different terms and even if each of us stands to gain very unequally from a particular transaction. In functional exchange transactions, unlike threat or grant transactions, we are all guaranteed to gain. This is one-half of the reason why exchange is the most efficient kind of economic transaction.

CHAPTER 6

Market Success

Getting to Know You.

The other half of the reason why exchange is the most efficient kind of economic transaction is that, since we all stand to gain from it, we tend to search each other out. The promise of increased satisfaction encourages potential exchangers to provide information about their needs and preferences and to seek such information from others. The more extensive and precise such information becomes, the more efficiently the exchangers with the most to gain from mutual exchanges do, in fact, find each other. In this way, goods and services will find their way into their most useful, most satisfaction producing applications, and the criteria for economic efficiency—that all resources, goods, and services are put to their "fittest", most productive use—are met.

Markets are institutions we have developed to facilitate this exchange of information and exchange of ownership. We often think of a market as a unique geographical place, such as a grocery store or a shopping center, where potential customers come to see the goods and services on open display, and where, when buyer and seller agree, these goods and services are physically delivered from one owner to another. But the transfer-or-exchange transformation is a nonphysical kind of transformation, and markets need not have a unique geographical location nor do they always require the physical delivery of goods and services. For example, looking in a catalogue and mailing in a check for something is also a market event, even though it takes place in your own home and even though the goods are not physically transfered at that time. Similarly, the American bond market consists of telephone conversations (mostly to bond brokers in New York City) about the ownership of nothing more substantial than promises to pay.

The existence of markets is often identified as the condition that defines a free enterprise economic system, which, indeed, is often synonymously called a market economy. True enough, open and accessible markets are a conspicuous characteristic of free enterprise economies, that is, economies that lean to individual rather than collective enterprise. But the transfer-and-exchange transformation exists in any economic system, and market exchange, which is an important part of this transformation in advanced economies, is also quite universal. In fact, the market is an important control center for any economy that is more than completely primitive, whether it leans toward free enterprise or towards collectivism. It is the cybernetic node of all the nerve endings that carry the myriad of messages back and forth between the consumption transformation and the preceding production and proprietary transformations. In a truly free enterprise economy (which exists in theory only), the market is allowed to function autonomously. In more collective and more centralized corporate economies, the controlling agencies—usual governmental economic planning agencies or corporate headquarters—monitor and intervene in the market process. They filter the signals, screen the responses, and they may add some information of their own. That is, in the theoretical free enterprise economy, the market is automatic, an "invisible hand" steering the ship of the economic state; in a more collective economy, it includes agencies of conscious and purposeful control, with somebody's quite visible hand on the tiller. In all economies, however, the market is the main center of control, subject, of course, to other controls that result from the decisions made in the other transformations, just as our brains are our bodily center of control, subject to "decisions" made elsewhere in our bodies by our hormones, our genetic code, and our other subsystems of control.

Money.

The establishment of a market is much more than just a degree of improvement in exchange efficiency. In fact, it provides the means for a quantum leap in the ultimate productivity of the entire economic sequence. And perhaps the most obvious of such means is money. With the existence of markets, money becomes useful for the first time as a common generalized measure and store of value. It also becomes the linguistic medium in which exchange transactions may be most effectively expressed. Through the use of money as a common denominator, the cost of all things exchanged in the market may be roughly compared. And through the use of money, we may store up our own individual funds of potential satisfactions—pools of purchasing power—without simultaneously having to make a specific proprietary claim on any particular resource or accumulation of goods and services. This convenience greatly encourages and facilitates such saving, simply because it allows time for eventually finding the most efficient use of the fund.

Money has so enhanced the economic process that even those transformations that in themselves find no expression in monetary terms are irretrievably altered by the existence of money and markets. The production transformation, which deals with the physical transformation of materials and energy, becomes exponentially more efficient through the specialization and the mass production made possible by the existence of a market-exchange transformation on a grand scale. Even a barter system would be completely inadequate to the task of integrating the specialized labor, materials, subassemblies, fuels, and industrial services that need to be mobilized and orchestrated in the modern production transformation. Likewise, the consumption transformation—also basically a physical transformation of materials and energies—would hardly be able to accept the quantity and diversity of consumer goods and services created by modern production if it had to articulate consumer demand in the economic deaf-mute's sign language of barter and non-monetary trade.

Thus, as the reach of the market extends from the local economy to the region, the nation, and eventually to the world of international trade, greater and more efficient levels of production and consumption specialization can be achieved. Consumers can articulate their individual preferences better, labor skills can become more refined and specialized, and machinery can be designed to focus more pointedly on specific subtasks. A much larger vista of the economic environment can be taken into rational consideration at once, so that less efficient applications of resources, materials, and energies may be exchanged for more efficient ones on a much larger scale. Modern technology can indulge itself fully in advanced mass production. The rigidities of established ownerships and performance patterns will be thawed and encouraged to flow dynamically into the most effective patterns, and the whole of the economy becomes much greater than the sum of its parts.

To be sure, all this is not an unmixed blessing. Because it allows the economic process to become much more round-about and complex, the distance between the proprietary and the consumption transformations is greatly lengthened by many intermediate market transformations. We, as individuals, are too often made to feel like an insignificant cog in some monstrous machine. All we can see is the small, specialized task that is our entire means of earning a living. We do not understand how we fit into the whole economic process, so we get little sense of personal identity from it. Furthermore, these specialized tasks are often numbing, repetitive drudgery. At higher levels of aggregation, regions and even nations may be tempted into such intense specialization that they lose their identity and sense of self to a dangerous degree. The well-being of whole populations in these monocultural economies becomes dependent on the market for coal, coffee, sugar, or whatever the specialty is. Chapter Seven will deal further with the problems created by the malfunctions and abuses of modern monetized and commercialized economies.

Prices.

Despite their drawbacks and malfunctions, large markets are essential to well-developed economies. Great quantities of materials, energies, goods, and services must change hands in the advanced economic process. To facilitate this exchange, the values of all commodities exchanged in market transactions are translated into the common denominator of money, and the ratio of the quantity of money to a commodity that expresses its value is called its *price*.

When people with opposite malproportions of accumulations approach each other in order to benefit mutually from a market exchange, the price is subject to negotiation. Many different techniques and rituals are used for price negotiation. One of the more familiar is an auction, in which the seller tries to find the most eager buyer by offering a limited quantity of a commodity for sale, first at a high price and then by lowering the offer price in small steps, until someone agrees to buy. Some auctions go in the opposite direction: the auctioneer keeps raising the price until there are no more willing buyers. The exchange is finally consummated with the party who offered the last and highest price. The advantage of this kind of auction to the auctioneer is that "the sky's the limit", especially when the bidders get excited and irrational. Auctions are still an important kind of market, not only in the sale of art objects, antiques, and used household goods, but also in the sale of real estate, agricultural produce, and investment stocks and bonds.

However, the item-by-item negotiation required by auction markets is too slow, tedious, and unpredictable for the vast majority of the commodities that must be moved along the economic sequence. For most kinds of commodity, a single price must be found that will achieve a "clearing" of the market, that is, result in the actual sale of all of that kind of commodity offered for sale. And this price level should be so satisfactory to both buyers and sellers that they would exchange again at that price, should the occasion arise, which, of course, it usually does in an ongoing economy.

In centrally controlled economies, the prices of many commodities, especially important ones, such as bread grains, meat, metals, fuels, housing, and clothing, are set by a governmental committee, control board, or similar agency. Statistical information about sales, inventories, shortages, production, and consumption guide the decisions of this agency. But other considerations and priorities can be important too, especially national defense, economic growth, income and wealth distribution, environmental protection, and public health and safety. Furthermore, in addition to setting prices, these agencies can often control the quantities of the commodities produced and sometimes even the quantities of the commodities consumed, so that their market regulating activities can use more than one tactic.

In free enterprise oriented economies, prices are generated by what economists call *demand and supply*. Demand is an aggregate expression of all the potential buyers' eagernesses and abilities to buy a commodity at any particular point in time. This buyers' demand is based mainly on the expected usefulness of the commodity in its intended function, that is, its expected usefulness in the production process or its expected usefulness in creating satisfactions. The demand for a commodity may also be influenced by fads and fashions, by legal restrictions and prohibitions, and by advertising.

Obviously, at a high price, a commodity will only be useful in very critical applications, and not many buyers will be able to afford it. As the price is lowered, more users and more buyers will be found for the commodity. For example, at the almost unthinkable price of one thousand dollars per gallon, we would find few buyers able to afford the water we are offering for sale from our well, and those who do buy at that price probably need the water to keep from dying of thirst, because they are lost in the middle of a desert. At the price of one tenth of a cent per gallon, almost everybody will buy our water, and they will use it for drinking, washing, and even sprinkling their lawns. Thus, at high prices, the quantity demanded will be low, and, at low prices, the quantity demanded will be high.

Likewise, the supply is an aggregate expression of all the potential sellers' eagernesses to sell a commodity. Sellers' supply is based mainly on the cost of producing the commodity, but it is also influenced by legal restrictions and prohibitions, such as those limiting the sales of alcoholic beverages in many states and localities. Only the few most efficient suppliers can sell profitably at a low price, and the aggregate quantity of a commodity supplied will be low. For example, if it is moderately costly to pump water out of our well, we would not want to sell any at a low price. As the price is increased, however, we will be able to begin to sell profitably. The original lowest-pumping-cost suppliers will be interested in expanding their sales, other less efficient well owners will want to join the business, and the aggregate quantity of water supplied will increase.

At first glance this seems to contradict both the familiar "cheaper by the dozen" sales pitch and the American faith in mass production, both of which seem to argue that the more is bought and more is produced for sale, the lower the price can be. But when a commodity is bought by the dozen instead of singly, it is essentially a different commodity. It has become a commodity that has to be stored in a holding tank or in the refrigerator, perhaps, and one that requires a larger single outlay of money at the point of purchase. It may be cheaper and more advantageous to buy by the dozen, but it may be as different a commodity from the single commodity as a pair of shoes is from a single shoe. The mass production of larger quantities of commodities often does create economies of scale, that is, more efficient production and lower priced commodities, but the length of time required to make the change into the sufficiently larger production runs that reap these rewards is usually counted in years or decades, even in the most rapidly developing economies.

This is a longer time span than is commonly included in an analysis of a particular market supply.

And so, as buyers demand more and more of a commodity as its price is decreased, while sellers supply less and less, a single price may be found at which the quantity demanded equals the quantity supplied. This is the *market price*. At this price, the market will be cleared, because all of that kind of commodity offered for sale is actually sold. By the definition of demand and supply, both buyers and sellers would exchange again at that price, should the occasion arise. Both benefit from the exchange.

Demand, supply, market price, and the actual quantity exchanged are neatly illustrated by the diagram in Figure I below, by which whole generations of economics students have been catechized. The horizontal axis delineates the quantities of a particular good or service offered for sale or offered to buy; the vertical axis delineates the offering price.

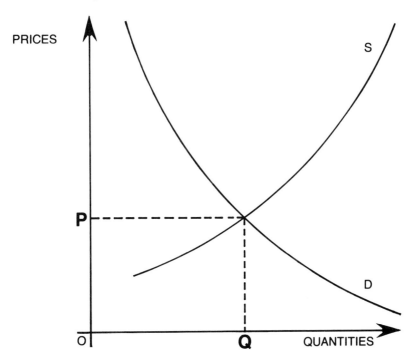

Figure I: Demand and Supply

The demanders' offers to buy are depicted by the demand curve, D (it is often drawn as a straight line); the suppliers' offers to sell are depicted by the supply curve, S (likewise often drawn as a straight line). The market price, P, and the actual quantity bought and sold, Q, are determined by the one point where the demanders and the suppliers agree on price and quantity: the point of intersection of the demand and supply curves.

Of course, many potential products seem unlikely ever to find a market price. Their demands and supplies do not intersect at any price level. For example, we may speculate that nuclear submarines will always be too expensive for private motor yacht racing and stucco bathtubs will always be too useless to anybody, no matter how low their price goes. Perhaps more important than such failure is the loss of opportunities incurred by the mass market even when it is successful. Because the market price, in both free enterprise and centrally controlled economies, is a single price for each single kind of commodity, many individual negotiations between individual buyers and sellers are bypassed. Buyers who find the market price too high, but who might have found a willing seller at a slightly lower price, had they been able to negotiate together individually (maybe with a small downward adjustment in the quality of the product), are often remorselessly locked out of the market. The mass market tends to sweep individual differences aside, forcing people to "take it or leave it" at the going market price. Its inherent efficiency gives it the power to impose a stern conformity on its subjects, the buyers and sellers, you and me.

CHAPTER 7

Market Failure

The Vulnerable Treadmill.

If markets are the key to the triumphs of modern economies, they are also the key to many of their troubles. The market may make possible a quantum leap in the efficiency and extent of economic activity, but its very existence means that there is another link in the economic sequence that may malfunction or fail. And the bigger this link, the greater the vulnerability.

The only economies that have approached even the appearance of long run constancy and stability have been the essentially nonmonetary economies, such as those of hunting and foraging societies, slash and burn moving agricultural tribes, and the monsoon rice paddy cultures. Market exchange is not very important in these stagnant economies, and usually the main new resources they require of their environment are simply solar energy and rainfall, neither of which require any economic management or effort. As appealing as it might seem to many of us who feel entrapped in the "rat race" of our modern and progressive world, we cannot turn the economic clock back to these earlier low productivity economies whose history marches to the beat of geologic time. Our population is already far too big to be supported by them, and we would not have enough to eat, let alone to be comfortable.

By contrast, the almost infinitely specialized labor force, producers, and consumers of a highly productive modern economy make for a precarious degree of interdependence. This interdependence is subject to major failure or malfunction caused by two tightly intertwined frailties common to all modern economies. One is the purposeful abuse, evasion, and restructuring of the economic system; the other is the potential instability of an advanced and complex market economy itself, that must "keep running faster, just to keep even". That is, new opportunities, new investments, new resources, and new technologies must constantly be developed, not only to provide economic sustenance for a growing population, but even just to maintain the per capita status quo in a rapidly changing world and to prevent the eventually diminishing returns of an economy that is stuck in a rut.

In a sense, this instability is not so much a malfunction—which would imply that it could be repaired—as it is the inherent vulnerability of a dynamic and alive system. It is a vulnerability that seems to increase not only with the complexity and interdependency of the economy but also with the productivity—the metabolism—of the economy. This appears to be a characteristic shared with all life processes that strive to succeed and thrive. The more they do, in fact, succeed, the more their metabolism—their utilization of the environment—intensifies, the more rapidly, perhaps, the entropic economic process leads to exhaustion, and the more urgently new opportunities must be found. This will be dealt with again at the end of Chapter Eight.

Inflation.

The two main symptoms of the vulnerability of the economic treadmill are inflation and unemployment. The inflationary problem is that money has hardly ever existed in the right amount to insure stable prices. Even the quantity of specie money, such as gold, which ought to be rather stable over the

long haul (and which is not a daily medium of exchange in
any major economy today), can change. It can be and was
easily lost, reminted into more but smaller coins, realloyed
with cheaper metals to stretch its quantity, lie unused, be
hidden in mattresses, or whatever. Not so easily today, but
certainly not impossibly, it can even be mined anew. Of
course, with our ordinary paper money and coins made of
cheap metals, the quantity of money can be changed with
much greater abandon, since only paper and book accounts,
rather than actual precious metal substances, are involved.
These so-called fiat moneys, which are used in all the major
economies of the world today, are simply notes and coins of
accepted value issued by a trusted source, such as the
government. The ratio of the quantity of this money offered
in the market exchange transformation relative to the quantity of goods and services offered has been unstable almost
everywhere in the world. And since the error is usually on
the side of too much money for too few commodities, the
main problem is inflation.

Not that a perfectly constant quantity of money is
desirable! Rather, a constant *ratio* of the quantity of money
offered for goods and services to the available quantity of
those goods and services is what is desired. This would
assure us of price stability and predictability in the market,
and it would make accumulations of money a safe way for us
to store up purchasing power and potential value. Without
this stability, we find that long-term market exchange contracts, such as life insurance policies and mortgages for the
purchase of homes, are more difficult to negotiate accurately.
Who knows what our money will be worth in the future?
Even shorter-term contracts, such as labor-management wage
agreements or eighteen month "easy payment plans" for the
purchase of a new car, are made less predictable when the
value of the monetary unit in which they are defined is
subject to unexpected changes. And, of course, our savings
accounts, savings bonds, certificates of deposit—all the possible accumulations in monetary form—may have an unex-
pectedly altered value when the ratio of money offered to
commodities offered is changed.

In both collectivist and free enterprise economies today, an unstable ratio is usually caused by the quantity of money growing more rapidly than the quantity of goods and services. Thus, each dollar, ruble, or lira will exchange for fewer and fewer goods and services, and inflation is created. One of the reasons why governments allow this condition to develop—or are unable to prevent it from developing—is the seductive appeal of deficit spending, that is, governments often spend more money than they take in from taxes. All economic actors, including individual persons, companies and corporations, collectives, communes, and governments, can occasionally spend more money than they take in, at least for a little while, by borrowing. But only governments, whose central banks happen also to be the sole issuer of the economy's currency, can arrange to make sure that there will be enough ready money to borrow, by having extra quantities of it printed. This is marvelously convenient, and the temptation to do so, given the popularity of government spending and the unpopularity of government taxing, is often irresistable.

The mechanism by which this works is that, when the government treasury spends more than it collects in taxes, it must borrow the money for this deficit expenditure through the sale of new issues of government securities to the public (mostly large corporations, commercial banks, investment funds, and wealthy institutions and individuals). The central bank—in the United States it is the Federal Reserve Bank—is prohibited from buying these securities directly from the government, but it is often concerned that all this new government borrowing does not dry up funds which would otherwise have gone to private industry. So it buys these government bonds and bills back from the public, by offering a good price for them. The catch is that the Federal Reserve Bank is always able to pay for the securities it buys, because these very same securities serve as the legal asset reserves that "back" the money it can issue. The result: the Federal Reserve Bank has new equal amounts of assets (the government securities) and liabilities (the Federal Rserve Notes— the money—it issued) on its books, the public has made a modest but quick profit by buying government securities from the Treasury and selling them to the Federal Reserve Bank at a better price, and the Treasury has been able to borrow newly created money to finance its deficit spending. Once completed, this circle can be run again and again.

Furthermore, government expenditures may be inflationary even if they are paid for by taxes and do not require new government borrowing. The reason is that many of the goods and services provided by the government do not contribute to economic satisfactions and, thus, to the productivity of the economic system. This is not to say that government supplied schools, roads, police, research, regulatory services, and such do not provide their full measure of satisfactions, but it is to say that another large part of government expenditure is economically narcissistic, serving needs created by the existence of governments. The most horrifying example is government military spending, which is necessitated by nothing other than the existence of other governments who are also spending militarily. Viewed in a global context, all this military hardware is economically quite unproductive, even destructive, whether used by the producing country itself or given as foreign aid. The technology that may trickle over to the domestic economy from innovations in military production is small compensation for the resources, vigor, and endogenous technology that the domestic economy is denied, as a consequence of the military emphasis. Nor do bombs and bullets contribute again to the economic sequence as useful goods and services; absolutely no one wants to be on the receiving end! Instead, all this acts as a leakage from the productive economy, draining away substance, but leaving the circulating money—and inflation—behind.

We may also wonder whether all the lawyers, lobbyists, clerks, staffers, functionaries, and commissars of our various bureaucracies do not feed more on self-justification than on economic reality. Working in the context of grant and threat transactions, the efficiency and accuracy with which these people are able to respond to the perceived needs of their constituencies is often less than satisfactory, which gives bureaucracy, in general, and government bureaucracies, in particular, an image of clumsy waste and high-handedness.

The Horizontal Class War.

And finally, inflation may just be human nature expressing itself in the monetary economy. You and I would certainly prefer receiving a higher wage to receiving a lower one, all other things being equal. And what farmer would not rather get a higher price than a lower one for his hogs? Obviously, unions push for higher wages for their members; just as obviously, corporations would prefer to receive as high a price for their products as possible, in order to maximize profits; and governments have always preferred more gold to less. The attempt to maximize money inflow is "situation normal" for almost every person, university department, corporation, club, government treasury, welfare agency, and so forth that has ever existed in a monetary economy. It is a motive that spans ideologies, cultures, geography, and the ages of history. Nobody likes to see his budget cut!

Ideally, this pressure to get more and more money is effectively countered by an equal and opposite resistance to being given more and more money. The buyers in the market, the tuition paying students, the purchasing agents of government agencies, the taxpayers, that is, all the people who spend money naturally want to spend as little as possible for what they get. They are driven by the same motive to maximize the amount of money owned, of course, and the result is that buyer and seller, payer and recipient settle the score by canceling each other out. So, whether through vigorous market competition in a free enterprise economy or through careful government regulation in a collectivist economy, an equalization of these forces is supposed to be assured.

Realistically, however, it is another story. The resistances that counter the drive for more and more money are often thwarted or bypassed. The larger businesses and government agencies grow, the less they have to submit passively to outside resistances. The objective economic disciplines of market competition and collectivist administrative efficiency easily devolve into subjective, collusive, and political expediences. And, instead of acting as checks and balances for each other, opposites often seem to attract. Unions and managements, government agencies and the industries they are supposed to regulate, purchasing offices and the suppliers with whom they deal often find that life is made very much easier when they "cooperate" with one another rather than resist each other in this money motive.

To the degree that these alliances are successful, they are able to divert larger money inflows to themselves than would be the case under conditions of a more objectively efficient economic discipline, and a new form of exploitation is born. This is not the traditional exploitation of the poor by the rich, the Marxist exploitation of the proletariat by the owners of the means of production, nor the racist exploitation of one color by another.* Rather, this exploitation is aimed at more inviting prospects, namely, others like us. It pits one union as much against other unions, whose negotiated wage increases must be matched or exceeded, as against management. It pits a national government's department of defense against that same government's other departments in a grasping for budgetary allocations, while its foreign adversary departments of defense become less foes to be feared than examples of budgetary abundance that must be imitated or exceeded at

---

*These traditional abuses may continue to be perceived in various economic contexts, but their economic justifications will have dwindled. After all, what great advantages can be milked out of the poor, out of unskilled "working stiffs", out of people who are merely differently colored or belonging to a minority today? They are hardly succulent prospects. Where we have failed to diagnose this accurately, we have prescribed the wrong cure. For example, the racial minorities and enclaves of rural poor in America are not being attacked by the middle class majority in a lusty orgy of monetary greed. Quite the contrary! They are being ignored. They are being moved away from, as businesses and residences flee from cities; they are being neglected, as services and innovations are addressed to the needs and preferences of the more affluent majority; and they are being forgotten, as their contribution to the standard of living of others is insufficient to gain them much attention.

home. It distracts corporate sales departments from their competitive mission against other firms, while they vie with their own product development or personnel departments for staff and funds. It allows a contractor to destroy excess production materials uselessly, in order to secure the continuation of a large allotment of these materials next year, and it fails to discourage the padding of executive expense accounts, because larger departmental disbursements set a better precedent than mere efficiency. In all the many large and small forms it takes, it is always an attempt by some alliance to channel money away from other similar alliances. In short, it is a kind of horizontal class war.

As economically perverse as all this may be, it still would not necessarily be inflationary if the money gains would equal the money losses. Indeed, if it were obviously such a zero-sum game, the players may even tire of it, recognizing its overall futility. But prominent among the players are those who can influence the supply of money, players such as government agencies, congressional committees, members of the financial and banking communities, and their many adjutants: the pressure groups, industrial lobbies, citizens collectives, and other special interest organizations. These actively interweave themselves into the horizontal class war, but with a difference; by influencing the government's expenditures and receipts and by influencing its monetary policies (almost always in the direction of more funds for their special projects and less taxes on their special interests), they exert a pressure for expanding the quantity of money available in the economic process. And when this expansion occurs more rapidly than the expansion of the quantity of goods and services offered for sale, inflation is the inevitable result.

Inflation may give the illusion of general economic gain. Since the tactics of the horizontal class war consist of trying to increase the inflow of money more rapidly than anyone else, it may appear that no one really loses, and some just win a little more than others. But, of course, only those who increase their inflow of money more rapidly than the inflationary average really gain; those who merely lag behind the average actually fall behind, in terms of real purchasing power. Workers on long-term wage contracts, such as teachers, nurses, and some government workers; all those who lend money, including particularly those whose meager savings are in savings bonds and savings accounts; retired people on pensions, anyone whose income and wealth is defined in fixed monetary terms; all suffer the full consequences of purchasing power lost through inflation. Meanwhile, speculators, money borrowers, people who can rapidly renegotiate their exchange contracts, and anyone holding wealth in real estate, stocks, and other nonmonetary forms, often escape. What this means it that, besides being unfair in any case, the disproportional impact of inflation usually burdens the lower income classes more heavily than the rich. The lower income people are the ones with the fixed incomes and with their savings invested in inflation-prone forms.

Obviously, the more thoroughly monetized an economy is, the more threatening the problem of inflation becomes. However, even under the worst of circumstances, various refuges and escape hatches are occasionally available. For example, by emphasizing activities that provide satisfactions for us directly, such as do-it-yourself entertainments, home repairs, and gardening, we can minimize monetary incomes and expenditures and sidestep the problem of inflation. Or perhaps we can arrange to earn a substantial part of our income in kind, as goods and services: a company car, use of a government agency's conference center as a vacation cabin, free access to the departmental Xerox machine (every little bit helps), or whatever. But all of this horizontal class war, all of these uneven effects of inflation and the resulting gyrations we go through to avoid inflation take their toll. They distort the economy, divert us from the directest paths to our economic satisfactions, and, in free enterprise oriented economies, they thwart the equilibrating forces of the market. Thus, they undercut economic efficiency and the wealth of the people. In this way, the horizontal class war turns out to be a *negative* sum game; total economic productivity is reduced because of it.

Unemployment.

The impact of unemployment is also cruelly disproportional and it too distorts the economy. But, before we praise employment and disparage unemployment without qualification, let us remember that we have already defined work as onerous and undesirable in Chapter Three, so lack of work should not always be considered a bad thing. In fact, a successful economic process should require as little work as possible. But, aside from that, work creates our income, and productive employment is the means by which a substantial part of total economic income is distributed among all of us. When the opportunities for productive employment are reduced, or, more precisely, when the *ratio* of productive employment opportunities to people desiring employment is reduced, without a compensating increase in other forms of productivity, economic growth regresses and the economic process contracts.

By itself, this is unfortunate enough, because a lower average standard of living results. But, as happens particularly in free enterprise oriented economies, when the resultant unemployment is not evenly distributed, but falls on a fraction of the workers—putting some individuals entirely out of work, while the remaining individuals still work full time —the unfairness and perversity of unemployment is fully felt by the unfortunate ones who bear the entire burden. Often this unfairness is further aggravated when unemployment strikes those who are already irrationally discriminated against, as is the case in race, sex, or age discrimination. In more collectivist societies, unemployment may be shared over a larger part of the labor force by arranging collectively to keep everyone employed, but at shorter hours. The resulting general *under*employment is still a waste of human resources, but, at least, the unfairness of disproportional unemployment is prevented or ameliorated.

All economies that are well monetized, whether they lean towards collectivism or free enterprise, are subject to unemployment. The reason is that money is a convenient store of value. It allows us to postpone the spending of our incomes; that is, it allows us to save. This is fine and proper on the individual level: "a penny saved is a penny earned", But it is most destabilizing when the aggregate saving by all the people in the economy increases, because goods are left unsold on the shelves and services are left without clients. Conversely, if aggregate saving should decrease, perhaps because people are now beginning to spend the money they saved too much of before, the shelves get bare and services become inadequate. If money were not available, such postponements would not be possible. All things produced would be much more likely to be immediately purchased, presumably in some form of barter exchange, and stability would prevail.

According to conventional, mostly Keynesian (named after English economist John Maynard Keynes [1883-1946]) analysis, unemployment is seen as the symptom of an

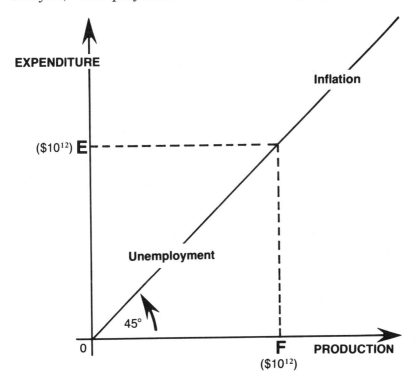

Figure J: The Keynesian Equilibrium

economy malfunctioning below optimum efficiency and inflation as the symptom of an economy malfunctioning above optimum efficiency. This is often depicted in a two dimensional graph, shown in Figure J below, in which an economy's aggregate production is delineated along the horizontal axis, and aggregate expenditure is delineated along the vertical axis. A forty-five degree angled diagonal vector line connects all the points at which production exactly equals expenditure. If, in the economy under consideration, full employment would create an aggregate production level in one year of F—which, let us say, represents an annual Gross National Product of one trillion (1,000,000,000,000 or 10^{12}) dollars—then aggregate expenditure that year would have to be at E, also one trillion dollars. Less than that much expenditure would create unsold goods on the shelves and, eventually, unemployment and slower production; more than that would create inflation, because more than one trillion dollars expenditure cannot induce more real production, since labor resources are already all fully employed at point F. The extra expenditure, then, is entirely taken up by rising prices, that is, by inflation.

So the trick is to balance the economy on the knife edge between unemployment on one side and inflation on the other, and this has been the point of view of most modern, free enterprise oriented economies since World War II. It is also the implicit balancing objective of collectivized planned economies. In recent years, however, inflation and unemployment have occurred simultaneously in many of the world's major market economies, and this Keynesian view has been seriously discredited. Nevertheless, the effort to minimize inflation and unemployment in these economies still consists mainly of governmental attempts to regulate the money supply, so that it will be just enough to promise full employment in production, but not so much that it will threaten inflation.

The governmental techniques for attempting to regulate the money supply include regulatory control of the banking industry, by which the ease of borrowing money can be influenced, and the deficit or surplus of its own budget accounts, by which the creation of new money is controlled. Augmenting these efforts, and of particular importance in centrally controlled collectivist economies, are the creation of employment opportunities by establishing government enterprises and direct control of prices and wages. Depending on the degree of collectivization in an economy, more direct matching of aggregate expenditures and production may be attempted. For example, the amounts of money individuals or families are allowed to save may be carefully controlled by the government, so as to prevent the accumulation of unsold goods. Indeed, even a matching of specific kinds of expenditures and production may be possible. For example, ordinary working people may be prohibited from buying imported goods, thus forcing them to buy domestically produced consumer goods. The instruments with which this matching is achieved are controlled resource allocation, production quotas, labor force placement, banking regulations, controlling access to markets, and the rationing of consumer goods and the services or even their direct distribution to the consumer. Regardless of method, however, success is not guaranteed. Inflation and unemployment continue to haunt the monetary economies. At best they can be minimized; at least they may be shared equitably by all the people in the economy; at worst they are merely disguised or accepted as natural and normal.

The Political Economics of Size.

The size of economic actors and of their collusive alliances has been a recurrent theme in much of the preceding discussion. Indeed, one of the more common charges leveled at modern economies is that they breed the concentration of economic power into larger and larger units, under which larger and larger numbers of people are aggregated and subsumed. Critics of industrialization speak of massification; critics of free enterprise economies speak of monopoly capitalism; and critics of collectivist economies speak of totalitarianism. Indeed, the very nature of all modern economies, with their sophisticated technologies, giant industrial units, commercialized agriculture, computerized managements, mass markets, and organized platoons of workers, lends itself uniquely to such concentrations. Out of practical necessity, decision making is always focused on a few economic leaders who decide for all of their constituents. The operation of General Motors must ultimately be the responsibility of the top management team. Similarly, the specific management of a large labor union, government agency, or university, no matter how carefully it is democratized for deciding general issues, must ultimately reside with its executives. To speak of economic freedom—the freedom of any individual, of you and me—to determine the behavior of such large units is to speak mainly in hopelessly optimistic terms.

Seen in this light, then, the concentrated powers are not so much the illegitimate fruit of conscious exploitation and abuse as they are the outgrowth of modern efficiency of the production and the transfer-or-exchange transformations. Perhaps, then, only lower levels of efficiency would have prevented these decision makers from growing as powerful and far reaching as they have in the advanced economies. (And none of us would favor lower efficiency and productivity, just to prevent a corporation or other economic agency from growing too big, would we?) But let us not be seduced by the temptation to claim that present conditions, whatever they are, by virtue of existing as they are, are normal and natural and, therefore, justified. This explanation would be too facile.

All I have said about collusion, the power of income, economic growth, and the horizontal class war argues that economic decision making units do consciously use tactics that concentrate power. Whether in free enterprise or collectivist economies, an effort to defend proprietary claims, to insure against unexpected changes, to exclude competitors, and to protect our own niche in the economic frieze is a part of predictable economic behavior. Not all of these tactics are economically endogenous and innocent responses to circumstances that have developed out of the economic process itself, such as reinvesting earned income to make an operation grow or taking advantage of technical efficiencies available only to larger operations. Many tactics are exogenous to the economy, purposely evasive of or artificially superimposed onto the economic process, in order to divert its course towards the intended concentration of economic power.

What these artificial tactics have in common is that they erect barriers that restrict the access to the protected economic activities. There are two ways of doing this: one is collusion. As we have already seen in Chapter Two, "What one of us may not be able to claim, because our claim is not powerful enough, may be successfully claimed by a conspiracy of similarly motivated individuals." Monopolies, trusts, exclusive franchises, cartells, sovereign areas of jurisdiction, blocs, spheres of influence, and other such descriptive terms are familiar and applicable in all modern economies. Untold numbers of "gentlemen's agreements" and convenient arrangements can accomplish the same end in a less formal way. And private licensing and accrediting arrangements that restrict the access of outsiders to various economic processes are arranged by collusive associations, such as the professional associations in higher education, medicine, and law, and by the closed or union shop contract between managements and unions. In many public and private instances, other results are also sought, such as assurance of quality, maintenance of market stability, protection from fraud, and avoidance of wasteful duplication of efforts. But, whatever the justification, artificial limitation of outsiders' freedom of access to available alternatives in the economic process is an important result.

The services of the government are also enlisted to secure the concentration of decision making powers. For example, the government may construct tariff and quota barriers against foreign competition, as it does for the textile industry in the United States; it may establish license and accreditation requirements for particular industries in order to restrict the entry of outsiders, as it does for such diverse industries as education and lobster fishing; or it may designate particular organizations as the sole agent, or monopolist, in one area of production, as it does for telephone services. Of course, governments and government departments and agencies are virtually the archetype of the collusive unit, since they are typically considered to embody the will of the collective. Even in free enterprise oriented economies, the national postal service is usually granted monopoly rights as an expression of a collective national priority. In more collectivist economies, such exclusivity is extended to many other government agencies in regard to their respective areas of operation.

The Power of Information.

The second way of artifically restricting access to economic activities is to restrict and to thwart the free flow of information. Information about new opportunities is kept secret, managerial and governmental economic decisions are made in strictest privacy, and technical information is jealously withheld from the public or effectively sterilized by the capture of exclusive rights to use this information through the rigorous application of patent and copyright laws.*

In some collectivist economies, the efforts to concentrate economic power goes beyond restricting the outflow of specific information to the point of restricting the freedom of the press and the freedom of information in general. This is usually considered to be more a political than an economic phenomenon, but the two are almost always inextricably intertwined. Freedom of speech and a free press often begin with the free communication of economic records and information about economic opportunities. The earliest writing on clay tablets discovered in the archeological digs of Babylon were not religious tracts, political manifestos, or even works of poetry; they were records of contracts, bills of sale, and receipts. At the other end of the historical continuum,

---

*Patent and copyright laws are usually justified on the basis that, without them, any new invention or creation could be immediately stolen by imitators, leaving the originator of the innovation with no way to profit from it and leaving potential innovators with no motive to innovate. By assuring some years of exclusive rights to an innovation, patents and copyrights probably do encourage innovation and progress. This writer, at least, is in favor of strong copyright laws.

the main use of communications satellites today is in transmitting signals for commerce, industry, and other economic
agencies. Literacy, accounting, universities, libraries, newspapers, and the mails and more recently the telephone,
television, and other media for telecommunication have
always found their main application in the economic process, although this is not to deny the importance of their
other uses. And, should political prohibitions of the freedoms of speech and expression be challenged, for example,
as they were in Czechoslovakia in the spring of 1968, the
challenge is likely to come from the economic sector that is
trying to increase the free flow of information.

Therefore, we often assume that the freedoms of information are part and parcel of those economies that lean
towards free enterprise. But, just as freedoms may be denied,
so they may be abused, and the main abuse is found in
advertising. Students of advertising often distinguish three
different functions in it, only one being unambiguously
socially and economically productive: the provision of information. Advertisements containing large amounts of pure
information, such as the classified ads in newspapers, can
only increase accuracy in decision making, by disseminating
information about available alternatives to large numbers of
people. Thus, they increase the efficiency of the economic
process and are generally to be encouraged.

But many advertisements also contain a second function, that of advocacy, which is intended to make people
decide in ways that are different from what they would have
done, had they been left unpropagandized. Indeed, any
advertisement that is more than a simple notice, unadorned
sign, or classified ad can only be justified on this ground.
That is, these advertisements try to get people to decide to
buy a product, relocate an industry, consider a career, and so
on in preference to their other alternatives. The advocacy
may be a well reasoned and honest attempt simply to "put
our best foot forward", but it is always an attempt to thwart
someone's unencumbered judgment. "Smoke Nicotinias,
they are mild!" may be the innocent expression of the
opinion of the enthusiastic producer of Nicotinia cigarettes,

but repeated thousands of times in billboards and magazines across the nation, it encites to the perversion of logic on a grand scale.

And when does "putting our best foot forward" become "telling little white lies"? And when does that become the third and illegitimate function of advertising: out and out fraud and deception? Especially since advertising is expensive and must be efficiently used, the temptation to "strike below the belt" informationally, to use psychological manipulation rather than reason and facts, to shave honesty a little close or simply to cheat is strong. An economic system that regularly leads us to this temptation is none the stronger for it.

By definition, only monopolistic competitors—those who enjoy exclusive domain in a part of the economy—can reap the harvests of their advertising, because they are the only ones who have access to these economic fields. Only General Motors Corporation and its dealers, who enjoy exclusive domain in the production and sales of new Chevrolet automobiles, find it useful to advertise new Chevrolets. Nonmonopolistic, freely competitive economic actors, such as wheat farmers in Nebraska, have no guarantee of exclusivity, because of the many actual and potential competitors have free and open access to their market. Under these circumstances, an advertiser would find himself advertising for all his competitors as well as for himself, which is not what he had intended to do. Since advertising is worthwhile only for monopolistic actors, it serves to indicate how large a proportion of the economy is, in fact, dominated by such actors and how large a proportion of the economy is subject to that kind of artificial barrier to free access. Obviously, in most modern economies, the proportion is very large.

But advertising is not merely a manifestation of concentration in an economy; it is also a cause of this concentration. The many national brands of consumer products that have pushed local brands off the shelves, conforming literally millions of individual consumers into single mass markets, could never have accomplished this prodigious feat without national advertising. And, admittedly, the efficiencies of mass production for such markets may not have been achieved either.

Economic Hyperactivity.

The "creation of new markets", which is often claimed by advertisers as an important success, is also an important indictment to be leveled against them, from the standpoint of economic efficiency. Dominating a person's thoughts with ideas that are powerfully favorable to one kind of economic activity tends to obfuscate the satisfactions that he may derive from all the other possible economic and noneconomic opportunities available to him. Being artificially conned into spending our money on some advertised purchase, we may be forced to work long hours (to earn the money for it) and to enjoy fewer hours of leisure than is optimal for us, according to our own preferences. To the degree that advertising is successful, we will have failed to maximize one of the basic decisions of our overall economic behavior.

By itself and in individual instances, this counter-productive aspect of advertising might be considered a small price to pay for the concommitant advantages of modern, technologically sophisiticated mass production. But when advertising is considered in toto, it is clear that a very substantial amount of economic materials and energies is misallocated. In the end, advertising can succeed in no way other than to push economic society onto a higher level of consumption of material goods and services than it would normally prefer. Therefore, advertising pushes society into greater demands on the environment, greater accumulations of owned resources, and greater expenditures of human energy on the economic process than would be the case if economic society could make its decisions according to its own best interests.

With the prevalence of the mass media of communication in modern societies, advertising becomes a part of the daily environment even for those people who are not themselves likely to be involved in that part of the economic process that is being advertised. Via newspapers and magazines, radio and television, and an incredible variety of outdoor advertising, modern free enterprise oriented societies are awash in advertising messages. Packaging and product design are also often made to carry a strong advertising message, leading to such dysfunctional aberrations as grotesquely decorated cereal boxes twice as big as their contents, fender fins on automobiles, and food coloring in toothpastes. Overconspicuous trademarks can make the public consumption of many products, from pants to pianos, into an essay in advertising. The hyperbole and stretching of the truth required in advertising becomes a malignancy throughout the society. It undermines the decency of the managers directly involved in creating the advertising, and it undermines the trust of the public in the goods and services sold, in business in general, and in the socioeconomic system in which they live, until even the highest level of leadership becomes infected. Perhaps because it must reach the vast majority of the population with information and advocacy about a mass produced commodity, advertising tends to aim at what the copy writers must perceive to be the lowest common denominator of taste. The result is that the substantive quality of advertising is often vulgar or even positively demeaning. Of course, this cheapening effect is difficult to measure, but it is powerful and should not be dismissed from the total evaluation of economic efficiency in providing the satisfactions of life for us.

Perhaps, then, we could turn to our governments for help after all. Instead of creating an overriding central control or state monopoly, perhaps the purpose of government programs, laws, and regulations could be to try to safeguard the individual's economic freedom of decision and to expand his access to economic opportunities, by limiting the concentration of economic power. Certainly this is already an important aspiration in the ideology of most of the so-called democratic socialisms of the noncommunist world today. This is also, to a greater or lesser degree, the purpose of antitrust legislation, resale price maintenance laws, subsidy programs for small businesses, environmental and consumer protection agencies, regulatory trade commissions, and some labor legislation in the more free enterprise oriented economies. Acting in the best interest of all the people, rather than merely in the best interest of a private monopolistic or other collusive group, the government could simply rule out advocative advertising and thus, prevent the resulting overconsumption, overproduction, pollution, irresponsible exhaustion of natural resources, and debasement of our economic life.

Unfortunately, however, these characteristics of modern economies seem to be quite persistent. The "three A's", Advertising, Affluence, and Americanization, seem to exert an attraction out of all proportion to their values. Even the underdeveloped and the collectivist economies tend to emulate the successes of the advanced, mostly free enterprise oriented economies, and, in the process, also adopt their malfunctions. It seems that governments are an inadequate line of defense. Perhaps it is unrealistic to expect collectivistic governmental means to come to the aid of individualistic ends.

CHAPTER **8**

Towards A
People Economics

The Poverty of Affluence.

The deeper we walk into it, the less we can "see the forest for the trees". Who would have guessed that whole nations of peoples, marching dutifully off to work an eight or more hour day, five or six days a week, about fifty weeks every year (allowing for a two week vacation), forty to fifty years of their adult lives, would be considered not nations of abject slaves, but nations of highly productive workers functioning in advanced and affluent economies? The small and often discredited voices of dissent heard from the hippie youth culture, from poets, bohemians, and from an occasional perceptive emissary from the not yet developed economies are drowned in the eager din of everybody else's commercial-industrial lockstep.

What task master is awful enough to impress these armies into such discipline? There are several possibilities. First and foremost, we must consider whether this full and voluntary participation in the modern affluent economic system is not simply the best rational choice among alternatives. Work is more attractive when it pays off handsomely, and, in these economies, it does pay off well. As we have seen in Figure F in Chapter Three, the higher the marginal returns from labor, the higher will be the opportunity cost imposed when work is neglected in favor of leisure. But we have also seen in Chapter Three, that there is an *income effect* that begins to operate at higher labor returns levels that makes leisure more attractive too. After all, we ought to have the time to enjoy our high productivity, as well as the time to earn it. And so it is not a foregone conclusion that a highly productive society must be a typical modern high work, high consumption society.

Perhaps, then, the taskmaster is that if we do not participate fully in this economy, we are not allowed to participate at all. As we have also seen in Chapter Three and again in Chapter Seven, few people in modern, industrialized economies are given the choice to work less and to consume less, according to their own needs and preferences. Some flexibility is being tried in a few industries, especially in the Scandinavian countries. But these are very much the exception to the rule. Try to tell your boss that you would prefer to work, let us say, only Monday and Wednesday mornings and all day Thursday. You will probably be told not to bother to come to work at all! So, at least, on an individual level, as far as you and I are concerned, this is a good reason to participate all the way. It would not be realistic for us to try to do otherwise.

In economies with a strong sense of national zeal for building and developing, hard work and high production becomes an end in itself. This is a phenomenon that seems to prevail particularly in economies that are already rapidly developing, and it is often the official stance taken by the leadership of collectivist economies. In these instances, social and even legal pressures to conform to the national purpose can override personal preferences, so this may be another good reason to participate.

Further enticing us into complete participation is the changing nature of consumption activities, which were once freely time consuming, but have become intensely time saving and money consuming in today's high production affluent societies. From archery to zen, equipment is becoming paramount in every leisure activity. The purpose is for us to consume better, quicker, and more. Outdoor activities, such as hunting, fishing, gardening, hiking, and swimming, which used to require mainly time and the proper geography, are now incomplete without a host of specialized ammunition, lures, boots, masks, and other often mechanized and motorized gear. Perhaps the extreme example may be modern camping in the designated campsites of our state and national parks, which now resembles an equipment manufacturers' exhibition more than a congregation of nature lovers. Athletics, always rather dependent on instruments and enclosures, have become a celebration of technological fireworks, in which new materials, electronic and mechanical advances, and even medical interventions can give the all-important competitive edge. Regarding indoor activities, the color television and hi fi sets, which cost hundreds—even thousands—of dollars, have almost completely replaced the 75 cent checker board and the zero-price games of charades. And, as if all this were not enough, we are even encouraged to double up our consumer spending, by buying phonograph records of music to eat by or to make love by and by installing stereo tape players and citizens' band radios in our automobiles to take-a-Sunday-drive by.

The object of all this is to cram as much consumption spending into as little time as possible. There are only 24 hours in every day, and the more rapidly we spend, the more time we will have left over to work to replenish our money. "Work hard, play hard", already a well established covenant of the protestant ethic, is imperceptibly translated into "Earn a lot, spend a lot." And, though a few of us may wonder at the futility of it all, most of us march along unquestioningly and even happily.

It is as if it were simply a natural characteristic of the modern economic process, a system in which money may be widely accepted as a measure of income and wealth. And, in the end, this may be the most powerful taskmaster of all. The proprietary transformation necessarily allocates most resources—most of the dimensions of time and space—to those uses that maximize money income and wealth. The enormous monetary reach of the market in the transfer-and-exchange transformation enables the production transformation to be marvelously efficient through extensive specialization and industrialization. The artificial aspects of advertising and collusion lead to powerful concentrations of decision making, which only exacerbate the tendency to substitute accountable money for the satisfactions of individual psychic income. And the predictable result will be the typical advanced, affluent, "Earn a lot, spend a lot" economy. As we have seen, it is often considered the natural coming-into-full-bloom of the developed economy and is eagerly emulated by the less developed economies. That the success of full development may, perhaps, be taken in another coin—a coin that pays more directly in terms of real satisfaction—seems hardly to cross anyone's mind.

Confirming this shortsightedness are the gaps in the affluence of most modern economies that serve to deceive us into believing that we can apparently afford no surcease from this total commitment to work and production. In the free enterprise oriented economies, there is often a paucity of those goods and services that are best supplied by the collective, such as the commodities of public health, education, and welfare. Highly paid and superbly trained private doctors working in miserably equipped and overcrowded public hospitals and mothers lined up in large, shiny, expensive cars to pick up their children from shabby, understaffed public schools are just two vignettes that are symbolic of this gap. In collectivist economies, the gap tends towards a paucity of goods provided by the private sector. A symbolic vignette that readily comes to mind here is the elegantly constructed four lane highway leading out of the capital city empty of automobile traffic. And in both kinds of economy there is a tendency for racial and ethnic minorities (in some cases, even majorities) to remain outside of the main advanced, affluent economic process. So the need for exertion, for more development, for more production is stressed and is believed and is acted upon.

More of this same kind of development and production, however, will not close these gaps. This lesson is being learned only with great difficulty, in spite of the obvious fact that a failed effort can seldom be corrected by repetition.

Each of these failures—these gaps—in every country, be it the failures of free enterprise or collectivism depicted in the vignettes above or be it the Eskimos in Canada, the Kazakhs of the Soviet Union, the Black minority in America, the majority of Blacks in the Union of South Africa, or even the women in suburbia, is unique and must be dealt with as a separate problem. Indeed, this uniqueness is what has kept these gaps open and unsolved. They are not susceptible to cure by more of the same; they cannot be filled by the mainstream economic process of their particular kind of economy. Only a less monolithic economy can come to grips with problems caused by diversity, heterogeneity, and nonconformity.

Overpopulation and Conformity.

When applied to the underdeveloped nations of the world, this diehard idea that the only possible direction for economic development is towards the typical industrial affluent state, is one of the most tragic misunderstandings of modern times. The sad list of errors committed in its name— including the glaring misapplication of technology, such as using bulldozers to build country lanes in Bangladesh; the misuse of investments, such as building steel mills and jet ports into rice paddy lands; and the misdirection of labor, such as conscripting tribesmen to work in mines and tempting the rural poor into already overcrowded cities—has become a familiar litany. But none of these is as diabolical as the effect of this kind of modernization on population growth in the underdeveloped countries.

The classical development of populations, the development that accompanied the drive to maturity of all the presently advanced, affluent economies, ran as follows: beginning with almost stable populations that had both a high birth and a high death rate, the first effects of economic development on population were a slightly increased birth rate and a dropping death rate. The reasons for the latter are clear; improved sanitation, more than any other single cultural advance, lowers death rates and lengthens life expectancies. The increase in the already high birth rates are less well understood, but probably the new opportunities found in the developing economies and, in the case of European populations, the new lands found in the Americas and elsewhere in the world, may have supplied the sense of promise and well-being that encourages family growth. In any case, with a high birth rate and a low death rate, the populations grew rapidly. With the accomplishment of industrialization, however, children ceased being valued as producer's goods, as "extra hands" in the shop or on the farm, and became consumer's goods, something to be enjoyed for their own sake, but, nevertheless, costly and a drain on the family budget. With this development, the birth rate began to drop, until, in the fully developed, affluent economies, it is about as low as the low death rate, resulting in stable, approximately "ZPG" (zero population growth) populations.

Helplessly, in full conformity to this classical pattern, the presently undeveloped countries have embarked on the same population development road. However, for them it can threaten to become the primrose path to perdition, because it is being taken in steps that are out of synchronization with one another. Sanitation, which can come very quickly and can often be as inexpensive as a simple change of handwashing habits, and which has often come at the behest of colonialists or rich foreign investors rather than developing in response to indigenous demand, has lowered death rates precipitously. Meanwhile, birth rates remain high, and the populations grow at an explosive tempo. At the same time, there is *not enough* accompanying industrialization and commercialization to assure everyone of a growing or even stable standard of living. There are no longer whole new continents into which the rapidly growing populations can overflow. Even food—*especially* food—often becomes inadequate, and the specter of destitution and starvation hovers perilously near.

The traditional hope is that, if only these nations could develop their economies quickly, their birth rates would soon go down in the usual classical response to industrialization, and they would have gotten over the untenable population explosion hump. The catch, of course, is that many new mouths created by their present rapid population growth are eating up the very resources and accumulations that would have been the building blocks of a more productive economy. So they are thoroughly checkmated; their populations grow too fast because they have a too high birth rate, they have a too high birth rate because they are economically underdeveloped, and they remain economically underdeveloped because their populations are growing too fast. The teachings of the good reverend Thomas Robert Malthus (1766-1834), that population, which grows at a geometric rate, will outgrow the food supply, which can only be increased at an arithmetic rate, appears to be coming true at last. But, in the absence of any alternative, the development policies of the nations caught in this trap continue to pin their fading hopes on eventually conforming to the classical pattern, and most of the foreign aid given to the underdeveloped countries since the end of World War II by the mature economies is likewise premised on this assumption.

All the evidence seems to indicate that they will fail. Even when considering those developing economies that are succeeding in making some improvements in their standard of living, the gap between them and the fully developed economies is often growing wider, not narrower. Therefore, the "revolution of rising expectations" in these countries is either leading to an overrapid consumption of the very resources and accumulations on which traditional economic development is based, or it is leading to increasing frustration, or—and this is most likely—it is leading to a combination of both. Furthermore, as we shall see below, our Planet Earth probably does not possess the natural resources to support a global affluence of the pattern developed in the advanced high productivity economies today. Would there be enough gasoline to fuel all the world's automobiles, if the Chinese, too, became two-car families? And, if there were, would not the resulting smog extend across the Pacific horizon to mingle with smog already blighting the air in California? But of course, most of this is idle conjecture, because in many undeveloped nations, the population trap remains the insuperable obstacle for the economic development that is envisioned in conformity with the classical pattern. In sum, then, it looks quite hopeless.

That is, it looks quite hopeless until we relinquish the dogma that population growth and economic development must follow the traditional classical patterns. When we have freed ourselves of this fixation, a variety of new alternatives become possible. Most important of them all, we may recognize that birth rates—called "child spacing behavior" by the professionals in family planning—are not exclusively a function of economic circumstances, condemning women in underdeveloped economies to a life of frequent births and numerous children. Of course, some of the old convention still holds true. The Malthusian calculus is necessarily still correct at the outer limits of the population growth rate, and it will put a lid on population growth no matter how high the birth rate. And, acting as a joint decision making unit, husbands and wives in developed economies will take economic motives into consideration when planning to restrict (more or less accurately) the size of their families. But, regardless of economic circumstances, if women were able to control the reproductive decision autonomously, there is every reason to believe that they would not champion the almost limitless motherhood and the high birth rates that are now considered normal and predictable in the underdeveloped countries.

In fact, this truth is ages old and is probably only recently as badly understood as it is. Even the Bible recognizes this truth when it decrees that "in sorrow" shall the fallen Eve "bring forth children". Pregnancy, parturition, nursing, and infant care, while they may give many moments of pleasure, must, on balance, be less than unmitigated joy for any woman. Motherhood itself, not to be belittled or denigrated in any way, does suffer from diminishing marginal returns, perhaps even more rapidly than many other experiences. Confirming this truth are the elaborate arrangements required to assure the continuation of the species in spite of it. For example, we seem to be genetically programmed to enjoy sex more than would seem necessary, if reproduction were not otherwise such a burden.* Further, the honor and sanctity with which almost all cultures fortify motherhood reveals its fragility; and the high social status earned by mothers (and sometimes fathers) of many children in some societies must be a kind of reimbursement for personal expenses incurred. If we turn back to Figure G and put ourselves into the place of a woman who is weighing having a baby against the alternatives, predicting the mental and physical cost to herself—the diapers, the two o'clock in the morning feedings, the years of care and worry—and imagining how the feedback from all this will feel, we will realize that to decide positively for reproduction we would either: (1) be very interested in achieving or reinforcing the status of motherhood: (2) be getting some significant social or material compensation for the act: or (3) be able to find no other alternatives.

Of course, throughout most of human history, women had little chance of weighing this decision, and there were not very many alternatives available to women anyway. They could declare complete chastity for themselves, perhaps by joining a religious order, or they could try any of a variety of mostly unreliable contraceptive devices and tactics. But, given the rigidities of traditional societies and the nature of the human animal, reproduction was usually the course of events. The effective contraceptives used a century or more now by people in the advanced and advancing economies are either used exclusively by men (the condom), require sophisticated male-female cooperation (the rhythm method), and/or require quite some gynecological sophistication, privacy, and clean running water, not to mention discipline and premeditation. While these may be effective means for responding to economic motives for family planning found in successfully developing or developed economies, they are not means subject to the exclusive administrative control of women themselves; therefore, they cannot be used to re-

---

*We need not formulate an hypothesis about it, but it does seem at first glance that sex is less behavior dominating in species in which pregnancy is short, which are not viviparous, and which do not care for their young.

spond to the most universal motives of all, the ages old feminine motives for the limitation of births described above.

Recently, however, all this has changed. The new contraceptive technology of "the Pill" and the intrauterine device (IUD) functions exclusively in the feminine decision context. It is likely that future contraceptives with less dangerous side effects will also be used exclusively in this context. With little sophistication and few of the accouterments of a richer economy, a woman can now respond to the decree that "in sorrow thou shalt bring forth children" by simply deciding to skip the whole thing. And, in one fell swoop, when the new contraceptives are accepted everywhere around the world, the population bomb could be defused. There is no reason to doubt their eventual acceptance. They do not require unattainable levels of sophistication or wealth either to produce or to consume. And, when we consider with what appalling rapidity the bottle feeding of infants is replacing breast feeding in even some of the poorest countries, at a considerable irrational economic loss and waste of vitality, we must realize that the rational use of these contraceptives, a similar, if much more beneficial, behavioral phenomenon, should also be accepted within the span of the next generation. Social rigidities and religious taboos do not last forever. And all this will have been achieved not by conforming to the prescriptions of conventional economic development, but by seeking progress through more directly individual means.

The Golden Age of Funded Resources.

And achieved it must be! Population growth cannot continue at present rates, for any of a number of very obvious reasons, all based on the limits of our Earth: the human race would end up "SRO", standing room only; we would pollute the environment to death; we would run out of resources; and, most specifically and most immediately, we would outgrow—and are outgrowing—the food supply. The recent popularization of this doomful point of view should not detract from its immutable logic. But none of this is new, for humans or for any other living species. As we have seen in Chapter Two, we have always tended to claim all the resources that are useful. Life's object is to live, to thrive, and to grow, and any population that is increasing itself, be it the population of piping plovers, the population of yellow perch, or even the population of poison ivy plants along the neighbor's fence line, must be celebrated or, at least, acknowledged for succeeding in doing something right and wasting no opportunities. Humans, who have been doubling their numbers every 35 years or so in this century, have obviously been doing very well for their species and have been wasting no opportunities.

Living "up to the hilt" does not have to mean reaching the limits where starvation and deprivation begin to take their toll. "God's Green Earth" is not covered with enfeebled masses of gasping fauna or endless thickets of pale and wilting flora. We do not completely understand the mechanisms of restraint that work to prevent such overreproduction or overpopulation, but it suffices to recognize that species that make this debilitating mistake will soon be replaced by more vigorous species that do not. Human beings have not yet been replaced, so why do we worry about the global population explosion? Have some new circumstances, perhaps, excluded us from the saving grace of a natural restraint that slows or stops our population growth before the cold calculus of resource limits visits destitution on our heads?

The answer is probably yes and no. No, we are no more threatened with totally debilitating overpopulation than any other species, even at the increased population densities projected for the next generation. I am convinced of no new or old behavior (or misbehavior) pattern that should cause us to suddenly burn ourselves out entirely as a species, like a prairie fire. What has changed is that there is hardly any group of people anywhere in the world today that is willing to accept the short life span and fifty-percent-plus infant mortality that usually accompanied an otherwise unrestrained reproductive behavior and population size throughout previous human history and that defines the overpopulation problem in the underdeveloped countries today. The revolution of rising expectations around the globe leads us to consider a reproduction success rate of fifty percent, which would be a singularly smashing success for a guppy and which was a familiar state of affairs for most of the humans who have ever lived, a cause for misery and despair now. Indeed, for those of us who have experienced better circumstances, this consideration can only appear fully justified.

And yes, we are facing a unique new danger of overpopulation caused by our living in the "Golden Age of Funded Resources." What has happened to us in the past two centuries is that some unique technological advances have fostered an unprecedented increase in productivity based on resources that exist only in limited funds on this earth. That is, the commercial-industrial-scientific-agricultural revolutions, which are causing the most extraordinary quantum jump in the economic effectiveness of human activity since the development of agriculture and civilization millennia ago, are based on bringing into use land, fossil fuels, and mineral deposits that have never been used before and that, once discovered, cannot be discovered again. Indeed, in the case of the fossil fuels and most of the minerals, once they have been used, they cannot even be used again. This is the way the entropy law, discussed in Chapter One, has come to haunt us. The new affluence in the fully developed economies, then, may not be so much a permanent step up to a better life as it is a temporary—very temporary, when viewed in geologic time—upward blip in our fortunes. Perhaps, we should be grateful for our good fortunes, however short they may be, for, although we may sense its coming, we will all be safely buried and gone before the dark side of the temporary blip begins to reappear. It is a problem for our children and our children's children more than it is for us.

Furthermore, perhaps this temporary fillip will provide the starting motor that will enable the economic engine to begin to operate on a new higher level, independent of any reliance on "not to be refilled or reused" resource funds. This is the hope of the optimists who believe that technological advances will solve all problems, including the serious population, resources, and environmental problems ushered in by this golden age. Without entangling ourselves in the controversy about this optimism, we can take note that such starting motors are not at all uncommon. A little cranking from outside is what gets many processes going, whether they be life processes, inorganic chemical reactions, or even economic processes. The surplus above subsistence provided by the funded resources, in which the advanced, affluent economies are luxuriating today, is also the stuff of which our scientific, exploratory, and technological advances are made. They would hardly be possible without it.

The question is whether or not these advances are turning in the correct direction to be able to perform as an effective starting motor. In order to succeed, these advances must emphasize the minimization of the use of energies and materials, the miniaturization of structures and equipment, and the concentration of the dispersed resources, such as hydrogen (for fuel), atmospheric nitrogen (for fertilizer), and solar energy, rather than the dispersion of the funded resources, as our traditional industrial technology is doing today. There is reason to hope that the advances will, in fact, lean in this direction. As we have seen in the demand and supply analysis in Chapter Six, as the supply of the funded resources and open environmental dumping grounds dwindles, the prices charged for it will begin—and have begun—to increase. This will stimulate the development of an alternate technology that will seek lower costs by concentrating on the dispersed resources and the minimization of wastes. Some recent technological developments in fields as diverse as electronics, housing construction, and manure management seem to have set off in this direction already.

A particularly fortunate aspect of many of these new advances is that they are knowledge centered rather than material or energy centered. That is, an increasingly important aspect of our commercial-industrial-scientific-agricultural revolutions is the scientific aspect. Of all our resources, knowledge is one that needs never to be economized, because it cannot be used up or exhausted. It provides a strongly egalitarian and democratic thrust for society, because it can be freely shared, and it is a major hope for future abundance, because it is itself virtually limitless. Economies that have cultivated and disseminated knowledge through intensive public education have been powerfully moved by this hopeful thrust, whether that was their conscious intent or not.

In spite of all these hopes, our Golden Age of Funded Resources still threatens to spring a horrifying trap on the human population. If the global population grows to the very limits of our present resource base, and no new economic engine is off and running when needed, the population will have to shrink back again when the funds run out. This, much more than immediate economic development, is the problem posed by the "third world" of rapidly increasing, economically underdeveloped populations. Scenarios of overlarge and dying populations desperately grasping for the last crumbs being hoarded by the once affluent nations cringing behind barricades of nuclear weapons are no less credible for being so ugly. And we can wonder whether traditional economic development, so accurately epitomized by the much vaunted Green Revolution in agriculture, which is heavily based on (exhaustible) petrochemical fertilizers, pesticides, and herbicides, does not increase, rather than decrease, the tension of this trap.

Some Alternatives.

None of which should be construed to suggest that we had best leave things as they are, because economic development can only make them worse. The way out of any problem is always progress, but what we need is progress of the right kind. Specifically, we now need to explore the direction of economic development that leads away from our heavy reliance on tangible industrial goods made from funded materials and fossil fuels. Many of these goods may not lend themselves to being transformed into consumer satisfactions as well as first imagined, anyway. It is almost too easy to point out that the cornucopia of motorbikes, radar ranges, disposable cigarette lighters, outboard motors, electric cocktail mixers, jet flights to Europe, and so on has not bought us happiness. (It is also almost too easy to point out that it is better to be rich and unhappy than poor and unhappy.) But it is a point well learned in Chapter Three that the law of eventually diminishing marginal returns operates seven days of every week, and the second camera, car, camper, or color TV is not as exciting as the first. In an affluent, advanced economy that bases its efficiency on techniques of mass production—the efficient duplication of products on an assembly line—there is also a tendency for us to have to take our wealth in the form of duplicates, and triplicates, or even worse. And the long arm of the law reaches out to diminish our returns.

We cannot predict exactly what the future will bring, but, under these circumstances the alternative will almost certainly involve meeting our needs and preferences more directly, with less reliance on homes-, garages-, and drivewaysful of industrial goods to serve as a mechanical priesthood of intermediaries between us and economic satisfaction. Some writers expect that a moral revolution, a "greening" of our psyches will have to take place in order to accomplish this. Indeed, if and when it is accomplished, it will probably appear clothed in such garb. But there will be a very rational and objective tendency to turn towards conservation and care of the environment, enjoyment of nature, satisfaction from being and doing, and disdain of mere material affluence, as pollution, the wanton destruction of nature, waste, and the ownership of material abundance becomes more and more expensive. Given the good common sense with which humanity avoids being overcharged, alternatives seem virtually inevitable.

But there are policies that can hasten the development of alternatives and prevent the lag in socioeconomic adjustments that is the root cause of so much pain and suffering accompanying change. As was already suggested in Chapter Two, ending the theft of our clean air, water, and serenity and placing a proper charge on these formerly free goods, would correct the illusion that many of the industrial products are produced at very low cost and are a marvelous bargain. Extending the legal rights of ownership to environmental zones other than land, already practiced to some degree, will have to become much more commonplace. This will not guarantee an immaculate (and, therefore, unproductive) world, but it will help in allowing us to weigh the advantages of production against its disadvantages more accurately.

Extending such property ownership is not a revolutionary change. Some critics, especially those who have a religious fervor about cleaning up the environment, will fault it for being far too establishmentarian. They will point out that property ownership—capitalism—itself has caused industrial excesses and that extending it even further seems an unlikely cure. But what our analysis has shown is that the industrial excesses are caused by *partial* property ownership, which is an invitation to cheating in the same way as a part-time marriage is. In fact, mainly *because* it is rather establishmentarian, extending individual and collective property ownership is a serious threat to the status quo. Unlike the more wildly revolutionary schemes, it will probably be implemented step by step, and it will cause major changes, none of which will be outrageously new and all of which are well tried and precedented. Of course, the defenders of the status quo realize this, and this is, perhaps, the main reason why the courts are so conservatively laggard in defending such extended property rights.

Another policy point of attack is against the manipulation and abuse of information. We may be well advised to apply "sunshine laws" more thoroughly to all organizations, private as well as governmental, that deal with the public. Again, this is not a revolutionary upturning of the normal situation. Corporations, unions, foundations, and many government agencies must already prepare a substantial account of their activities for the public record. Extending this practice, especially into the arena of their advertising and public relations, would not be a new and unprecedented approach. Of course, all of this requires substantial freedom of the press, which, sadly, is a freedom that is not gaining around the world. Particularly in the dogmatically collectivist economies, the accompanying political stance is many dark ages away from the sunshine of freely flowing and honest information.

A very specific policy suggestion, one that is a combination of extending property rights and extending informational efficiency, would be for the citizens collectively to make a more powerful proprietary claim over their radio and television airwaves. This is not a guaranteed cure, but it has possibilities. In most collectivist economies—and some not even very collectivist—the broadcast media are already claimed by the government in the name of the people, and the results are mixed, from the best of BBC to the worst of Radio Tirana. In the United States, licenses to use these airwaves are granted to private organizations for a very minimal fee. Granted cheaply and with a minimum of controls, these licenses can be used for little else but commercial hucksterism and the simplest excitements that can reach over the highest mental thresholds. Anything more demanding could not compete in a media dedicated rather exclusively to serving mass production and mass marketing interests. This encourages an extraordinary dulling of informational flow, in both the programming and the advertising, that calls the basic veracity of the entire broadcast media into question and seriously undermines the credibility of the entire social, economic, and political system, to say nothing of the infamous "cultural wasteland" it creates. A few more public TV channels and a few more public radio stations may work wonders in attracting people away from the commercial-industrial sights and sounds and toward a better alternative.

Broadcast advertising is often the most abusive of such information flows, because it tends to carry the minimum of information and the maximum of the puffery that will thwart the accuracy of consumer decision making. As the cost of this abuse increases in an increasingly massified and industrialized world, we can expect the direct regulation of the content of advertising also to increase, on the principle that

"The most stringent protection of free speech would not protect a man in falsely shouting fire in a theater . . .", especially, we might add, when the theater is getting more and more crowded and freedom of movement more and more restricted. Perhaps an attractive alternative or amendment to this policy would be to disallow more than a certain percentage of gross sales to be written off from taxable income as advertising expenses. Adjusted to the needs of different industries, this may help to dry out the deluge of advertising that is making our society conform blindly to the demands of mass production and mass consumption. And this is also a nonrevolutionary and well precedented approach. We have often attempted and sometimes succeeded in limiting what may be considered a legitimate cost of doing business, whether this is propagandizing a product, supporting a political party, going on a congressional junket to Paris to "study" their tourist industry, or taking a patient to lunch.

A policy that would favor decision makers who account the distant future into the outcomes of their decisions would help powerfully in developing economic alternatives that would treat the environment with a new found sense of long-run responsibility. We have seen in Chapter Three that the family structure especially cultivates decision horizons that go beyond the usual few years, even to several generations hence. According to this analysis, for example, we would expect family farms to be more concerned about the effect of chemical fertilizers, pesticides, and herbicides on the very long-run fertility of their homestead than would be the incorporated agribusinesses that manage an increasing proportion of our agriculture for efficient commerce and maximum profits today. Good statistics dealing with this comparison are not available, but if we can believe what is published about organic farming and responsible agriculture, it does seem to be very much a family affair.

As the distance between the farm field and our dinner table grows longer in both miles and time, due to the increased industrialization and commercialization of agriculture, as the advanced and affluent nations are becoming more and more overfed and undernourished, as we become

captives of the less and less varied, the more heavily processed, and the increasingly altered and adulterated foods we
buy in supermarkets and quick meal franchises, the costs of
short decision horizons on the farm become more obviously
burdensome. Tax policies, which now generally favor the
corporate structure in doing all kinds of business, might be
rewritten beneficially to favor family held enterprises.

Some economists point out that the gradual increase in
the importance of the service sector of the economy—the
communication, transportation, health, education, welfare,
recreation, and similar industries—that accompanies the
maturation of advanced economies is a harbinger of a greater
range of diversity and available alternatives. Services do not
rely on the heavy use of materials and energies as much as
goods do, nor are they as susceptible to the efficiencies of
mass production. Indeed, really effective services, be they
expert surgery, hair dressing, teaching, or whatever, are often
premised on a very personal relationship between the producer and consumer. This individualization naturally tends
to counter an advanced economy's predilection for
homogeneity in its products and conformity in its consumers. A full pricing of all goods and services, a pricing that
includes also the costs of using the environment, as
suggested earlier in this section, would make the services
relatively less expensive and would encourage a switch away
from the goods that rely on the heavy use of materials and
energies. And again, often consisting of smaller and family
held firms, the services sector would be expected to benefit
from tax reforms that correct the favoritism enjoyed by
corporations and would be expected to cultivate larger
decision horizons than other organizations, if the competition or collective economic decisions would allow them to
do so.

Education, as we have seen in Chapter Four, is the main
instrument for discovering and developing new alternatives.
Simply learning that economic progress need not always take
the form of increased material production, massification, and
the intensive consumption of the funded resources is a big
step forward. "Diagnosis is half the cure." It may even be

more than half the cure. Socioanalysis, like psychoanalysis, may effect most of the cure merely by dredging up the suppressed memories into full consciousness. All of which does not mean that the task is much simplified, however. How many people, how many leaders in both developed and less developed economies still understand progress to mean only more, bigger, and faster material consumption?

By developing the creative genius of individuals and by giving them the means to express themselves, education is the single greatest threat to bland homogeneity and mindless conformity. Perhaps realizing this intuitively, perhaps merely as a result of seeking efficiency in public schooling, education in all advanced, affluent economies appears to be organized in a way that obstructs the flowering of individualism. From kindergarten through the formal defense of the doctoral dissertation, the modern educational lockstep stresses adjustment to the group, standardization, and normalization (in the sense of establishing norms, as in "Normal School"). Even in later professional life, such social instruments as licensing, accreditation, professional memberships, and peer reviews can be used to impress conformity. Some critics have charged that the entire educational structure is a diabolical scheme to provide the captains of industry with a population of docile workers and salivating mass consumers. Other critics call for a "deschooling" of society, not to bring darkness to where there once was light, but, on the contrary, to allow individual sparkling brilliance where once only a feeble homogeneous group glow was permitted.

We will not take up the cudgels of educational controversy here, except to note that many new developments in education point towards decentralization and diversity. The new information storage, retrieval, transmission, and duplication devices can work to liberate individuals and far flung learning centers from both their isolation and their monogenous dependence on the large, well established, usually urban universities, libraries, and research institutes. The various techniques and machines for individually paced learning, still used almost entirely to serve up a massified and standardized curriculum today, may in the future provide the means for radically diversifying and individualizing the subject matter being learned.

The pressures for consolidation of schools, standardization of tests, and the organization of "megaversities" that built so powerfully after World War II may have spent themselves and may be replaced by a renaissance of concern for local needs, preferences, and contributions. Various "free schools" and "alternative schools" from kindergarten through college levels have separated themselves from the traditional institutions purposely, in order to pursue differing educational emphases. Centers for research into and the dissemination of "appropriate technologies" are being established purposely as a counterweight to big corporation technology and big university science. A healthy diversity of public and private higher education is an accepted policy goal of many state governments and boards of regents. But mostly the education system is a reflection of the socioeconomic reality of the day. As new alternatives are developed in the economy, the homogenous educational lockstep will also break up into new rhythms and new music.

Diversity, Evolution, and Ideology Again.

Beyond providing our "daily bread", the main responsibility of the economic system is to respond to the constantly changing environment in such a way that our survival—and preferably our thriving, successful survival—is assured. In all populations of living things, the main way this is achieved is by diversity. That is, enough genetic, behavioral, and/or social diversity exists within a species so that those forms that are particularly well adapted to the new conditions will be rewarded by success and survival, while those that happen to fail will soon cease to exist and cease to burden the population. And thus, the evolution of economic society, the development of economic reality is also based on the prerequisite existence of diversity within the economy.

Evolutionary theory is not without its detractors, many of whom do not necessarily live in the American "Bible

Belt". One cause of misgiving about evolution is its archly secular emphasis. It tends to demystify life with a vengeance. Certainly the irresponsibility, immorality, and even the brutal nihilism that has been excused in the name of necessary evolutionary change have turned many against the entire concept. Others are repelled by its automatic and mathematically random inevitability. And still others disagree with its mechanics. They argue that diversity, rather than being a guarantee of survival, is a costly inefficiency that is, at best, an unnecessary diversion, and, at worst, a purposeful subversion.

This latter opposition to evolution is well typified by Marxist "scientific communism", in which the easily accepted scientific proposition, that only one scientifically correct answer exists for any one question, is extended to the entire society, where it comes to mean that only one solution—and that would, of course, be the Communist Party solution—exists for any socioeconomic problem. The thorough squelching of all differences of opinion and diversities of practice that results in communist countries which follow this dictate results in the totalitarian state that has become so dreadfully familiar in the latter half of this twentieth century. Much less totalitarian, but similarly monolithic, the massification of production and consumption in the advanced, free enterprise oriented economies also works out to one "best solution" to vastly aggregated and averaged economic problems. We have come a long way from Henry Ford's dictum that the buyers of his first mass produced Model T's could choose any color they preferred, "so long as it's black." But even today, it is difficult in these economies to choose *not* to run a car at all, *not* to work from nine to five every day, *not* to eat heavily processed and altered foods, and so on and on.

The idea that a single, best solution to a socioeconomic problem is possible to find is based on two assumptions: one, that a collective can speak effectively for all the individuals in its constituency on the matter at issue, and, two, that the collective can anticipate the problems of the future and can accurately predict which of the available alternatives will have the best outcome. The entire ideological issue between collectivism and individualism is capsulated in the question about whether or not these two basic assumptions hold. If, indeed, a collective organization can meet these two assumptions, it would certainly be the most direct, most efficient way of surviving and thriving. Instead of squandering materials, energies, time, and life on ineffective and wasteful deviations—trials and errors—the one true course could be steered immediately by all together and collectively. If, however, one of the assumptions is not met, if the collective does not represent all of its members' needs and preferences accurately or if it is mistaken about the future, then it becomes a ship of fools, sailing straight for trouble or disaster.

Obviously no one ideological dogma, collectivist or individualist-free enterprise, is automatically always best. If the problem to be solved is basic, such as adequate staple food, medical care, or security against foreign attack, then a collective may speak quite accurately in unison with all its constituents. Likewise if the futurity of a problem is short and manageably predictable, such as predicting the outcomes of alternate irrigation systems or alternate techniques of harvesting crops, then decisions made by large organizations in the name of a collective have a good chance of being accurate and efficient. Indeed, the primitive economies of preindustrial tribes and clans that produce only the most basic needs and face only the most immediate problems in a purposeful way are often strongly collectivist. But, as economies become more advanced, they soon can afford to range into the kinds of production and consumption that are less concerned with common staples and more subject to differing personal preferences. And, as they become more advanced, they also encroach further and further into the entire entropic process of their environment. The decision horizons required for the biggest problems they face approach eternity or, at least, several generations into the future. Whether any large collective, managed, as it must be, by a complex bureaucracy, is capable of cultivating such a large decision horizon and keeping it flexible and dynamically responsive to changing reality, is doubtful. At least, past experience seems to indicate so.

All of which is to say that the choice between collectivism and individualistic free enterprise is not simply a matter of ideological preference. It is a critical matter of choosing the right organization for the right job. Collective structures should be used where they can do the job most efficiently, where they represent the preferences of their constituents accurately, and where they can maintain an adequately responsible decision horizon. More diverse individualistic structures could be used when the collectives fail to meet the above conditions, when individual needs and preferences cannot be aggregated effectively, and when the future is so unclear that we had "better not put all our eggs into one basket". Perhaps this simple logic explains why all economies of all ideological persuasions are still mixed, containing both collective and more individualized participant structures: they have merely assigned the right structure to the right task, all safely within the context of the economy's ideological slant, of course.

But I have misgiving about this pat answer. It seems to be more easily said than done, because it does not jibe completely with reality. A glance around the various economies of the world shows too many sick and malfunctioning railroads, corporate manufacturers, departments of agriculture, postal services, collective farms, transit authorities, special purpose communes, families, and so on. These cannot make the claim that the right organization has gravitated towards the right job. Nor does this concept hold up theoretically. Consider that the ultimate socioeconomic arbiter of the best structure in any particular case has to be a process akin to what biologists call natural selection. "The proof of the pudding is in the tasting," we might say. In order to function effectively, this process depends on a constantly (automatically and randomly) renewed diversity, so that it can select the optimum among alternatives accurately. And that brings us right back to diversity as the key to economic success and survival, which is theoretically contrary to the concept of an intentionally determined choice of structural form. Finally, what we have learned earlier in this chapter about the artificial means of subverting decision making and what we have learned in Chapter Four about the power of income indicates that, once established, collusive or collective organizations will use many natural and artificial means to try to survive and succeed. As a result, these entities are able to outgrow and outlive their most efficient usefulness and are able to thwart the further process of naturally selecting the best organizational form.

In the end, we seem to be left with economies whose collective or individualistic structures are assigned by a combination of historical accident and vested interests, all enshrouded in a thick haze of ideological prejudice. A worse prescription for meeting the needs of a rapidly changing and largely unpredictable future can hardly be imagined. Most societies seem to be, at least, implicitly aware of this and have developed some techniques to deal with the problem. One such technique is to entertain recurring "throw the rascals out" purges. More publicized in politics and government than in business, but certainly quite common in all organizations and in all economies, such revolutions (or, at least, "palace revolutions") are useful not only to replace no longer efficient personnel, but also as an opportunity to rebuild organizations into more efficient structures. Formalizing these purges, as is done in those countries that hold periodic elections, may benefit the efficiency of many kinds of organizations, including especially the large, bureaucratic, collective corporate and socialist economic organizations throughout the world. So far, a compulsory retirement age in industry, rotating department chairmanships in universities, and other such mild devices are the closest most of these organizations come to formal means for freshening up their ranks and their structures. Much more could be done.

Another societal response to deal with organizational forms that meet neither the people's needs and preferences nor the changing future successfully is to develop an antipathy towards bigness in general. "Big government", "big business", "big labor", the "military-industrial complex", the "syndicate", "big brother", and "technology"—when the term is used pejoratively—are respectively government, business, unions, armies and their suppliers, criminals, collective leadership, and applied science, all made especially suspect and sinister by being called "big". Free enterprise leaning economies develop governmental anti-trust policies, collectivists inveigh against giant monopoly capitalists, minorities celebrate their separate ethnicity, and those that fall in between these categories proselytize for a world in which "small is beautiful". Surprisingly, these broadsides against bigness often come quite close to the mark. Given the nature of bureaucracy, the larger the organization is, the more difficult a dynamic and flexible response to individual needs and preferences and to changing environmental conditions becomes. Bigness is an index of real or potential economic inefficiency.*

One way of limiting these excesses of bigness would be to extend the formal concept of death to organizations, such as corporations, collectives, government agencies, and communes, that, unlike real human individuals, presently enjoy a potentially unlimited life-span. In some cases, particularly those depending on government funding, this can be accomplished through "zero base budgeting", in which the annual (or biennial or even longer spaced) appropriations for the organization must be entirely justified, from zero dollars up, rather than requiring justification only for the annual changes (read: increases) in the budget. This practice institutionalizes a periodic review of the justification for the entire organization itself. And it simplifies the organization's death: the *coup de grace* is delivered passively merely by refusing funds.

Another way organizational immortality can be avoided is to limit the time span of chartered organizations. Practiced

---

*This definition certainly contradicts the concept first developed in Chapter Four that growth (bigness) is the result of success in the economic process. In fact, that first concept still holds. Growth is still a response to success. But, as we have seen especially in this and the last chapter, many economic organizations functioning in modern, advanced, economies are able to grow and maintain their bigness by collusion and the economically artificial and exploitive means of advertising and information control. In that case, their efficiency and success is fraudulent, when seen from the perspective of the economic process as a whole.

as a matter of course centuries ago, when incorporation was a new structural invention and corporations were chartered for a limited time only, the idea was recently reintroduced as a "sunset law" that automatically limits the life-span of government agencies. This idea could also be easily reapplied to corporations, perhaps, especially to those that exceed a certain size. Renewal of their charters could be made contingent on their demonstrable ability to function effectively in the economic process without depending on the crutches of heavy advertising, information control, and collusion. Not that General Motors or Standard Oil would have to close up shop every five years or so, but their economic effectiveness could be reviewed, and their permission to issue new stock, to merge with other corporations, to branch out into new industries, and to remain incorporated as one single organization could be reconsidered.

Precedents or near precedents exist for both of these techniques. Zero base budgeting has been used by some governments, with great success and effectiveness. Limited time span licenses and charters which require justification for renewal are already a way of life in many economic activities. Applying these concepts to new purposes and to other kinds of organizations, therefore, is not radical or revolutionary, which, of course, makes them especially threatening to the vested interests of the status quo. Great care must be exercised to prevent the agencies—probably government agencies—that administer and regulate these programs from themselves becoming centers of collusion, deception, and arbitrary power. Again we may wonder whether collective means can be used to further individual and diversifying ends. But, under good circumstances, with much citizen participation, with good and freely flowing information, and with good people at the helm, chances are also good that these programs would stimulate a great increase in the diversity of organizations with which an economy serves its people and bravely tries to find new paths along which to meet its future best.

Freedom and Entropy.

New paths must be found. The old, well trodden ones soon lead to diminishing returns, to exhaustion, and to entropy. Not only our present well-being, but also our future survival depends on a dynamic, positive thrust for innovation, discovery, and development. But more than that, the economic basis for freedom also depends on the same thrust.

The old, conventional, mechanistic view of the economy, in which the flows of goods and money were circular and equilibria tended to be self-establishing and self-correcting, is no longer realistic. The economy is not a recirculating *perpetuum mobile* off in a vacuum. Rather it is, in fact, a class of organic and inorganic chemical reactions, steered by the human life process, that—like all chemical reactions—is careening towards entropy. This is a one way street, a characteristic better illustrated by Figures A and B in Chapter One than by the usual circular flow diagrams that dress out the conventional economics textbooks. And this means two very important things to us: one, that, unless we find new paths, new streets, we will soon reach the end of the entropic line; and two, that such equilibria as may exist must be very temporary and very partial, because the only lasting equilibrium is final exhaustion and dispersal.

Like saying that "in the long-run, we are all dead", emphasizing that the economic process is unstable and ultimately entropic may sound grim and pessimistic. For many environmentalists, panicked by our dwindling funded resources, our cancerously growing pollution, and our exploding population, this grim message is indeed a binding cease and desist order. They would have the human race stop all economic activities that leave any tracks at all, that are not absolutely recyclable and self-contained, as if such ideally nonentropic processes were even possible.

But the message is quite the opposite. It is our hope, our declaration of freedom! This instability and indeterminateness of the entropic economic process means the final answer need never be pronounced. It provides the ever changing environment in which we can find the opportunities to escape the traps of circularity and the mechanical equilibria that would otherwise have turned us into robots in our lifetimes. It enables us to discover new paths and new horizons and gives us the freedom to use our dimensions of time and space in new ways, not as refined automata, finally engineered to function at some artificial measure of maximum efficiency, but as unpredictable, renewable, diverse, seeking, striving, living (and dying) organisms. This real freedom is the freedom that underlies all others, without which political, religious, and intellectual freedoms soon become an illusion. In the end, this freedom is the nature and root cause of the wealth of people.

Index